The MAN *Who* CHANGED EVERYTHING

The Life of James Clerk Maxwell

Basil Mahon

WILEY

Published in the UK in 2003 by John Wiley & Sons Ltd, The Atrium, Southern Gate,
Chichester, West Sussex PO19 8SQ, England
Telephone (+44) 1243 779777

Email (for orders and customer service enquiries): cs-books@wiley.co.uk
Visit our Home Page on www.wileyeurope.com or www.wiley.com

Reprinted October 2003

Other Wiley Editorial Offices

John Wiley & Sons Inc., 111 River Street, Hoboken, NJ 07030, USA

Jossey-Bass, 989 Market Street, San Francisco, CA 94103-1741, USA

Wiley-VCH Verlag GmbH, Boschstr. 12, D-69469 Weinheim, Germany

John Wiley & Sons Australia Ltd, 33 Park Road, Milton, Queensland 4064, Australia

John Wiley & Sons (Asia) Pte Ltd, 2 Clementi Loop #02-01, Jin Xing Distripark, Singapore 129809

John Wiley & Sons Canada Ltd, 22 Worcester Road, Etobicoke, Ontario, Canada M9W 1L1

Wiley also publishes its books in a variety of electronic formats. Some content that appears in print may not be available in electronic books.

British Library Cataloguing in Publication Data

A catalogue record for this book is available from the British Library

ISBN 0-470-86088-X

Typeset in $10\frac{1}{2}/13\frac{1}{2}$pt Photina by Mathematical Composition Setters Ltd, Salisbury, Wiltshire
Printed and bound in Great Britain by The Cromwell Press, Trowbridge, Wiltshire
This book is printed on acid-free paper responsibly manufactured from sustainable forestry in which at least two trees are planted for each one used for paper production.

The MAN *Who* CHANGED EVERYTHING

James Clerk Maxwell. From a bronze bust by Charles D'Orville Pilkington Jackson. Courtesy of the University of Aberdeen

DEDICATION

To Ann

CONTENTS

LIST OF ILLUSTRATIONS

PREFACE

I fell under Maxwell's spell when I was about 16 but for more than 40 years he was a man of mystery. His name cropped up in all the popular accounts of twentieth century discoveries such as relativity and quantum theory, and when I became an engineering student I learnt that his equations were the fount of all knowledge in electromagnetism. They seemed to work by magic—something I attributed, with good grounds, to imperfect understanding. But now that I understand the equations a little better they seem even more magical.

Over the years the spell tightened its grip. My extensive, if desultory, reading on scientific matters served to deepen the mystery. Usually introduced as 'the great James Clerk Maxwell', his influence on the physical sciences seemed to be all-pervasive. Yet he was scarcely known in the wider world; most of my friends and colleagues had never heard of him, although all knew of Newton and Einstein and most knew of Faraday. What is more, nothing in what I had read revealed much about Maxwell's life beyond the bare facts that he was Scottish and lived in the mid-nineteenth century.

The time had come to unravel the mystery. A few years ago I looked him up in all the reference books I could find, starting in the local library. The *Encyclopaedia Britannica* had a helpful 2000 word entry and a short bibliography. It was like finding the way to a store of buried treasure. Maxwell was not only one of the most brilliant and influential scientists who ever lived but an altogether fine and engaging man. And he seemed to inspire in writers a unique combination of wonder and affection; a *Times Literary Supplement* editorial of 1925, preserved in Trinity College Library, sums it up by saying that Maxwell was 'to physicists, easily the most magical figure of the nineteenth century'.

I have tried to tell the story simply and directly, putting the reader at Maxwell's side, seeing the world from his perspective as his life unfolds. Hence the main narrative contains few references to sources and no more background or detail than is needed for the story. The separate Notes section attends to these aspects and gives some interesting sidelights.

To his friends, and he had many, Maxwell was the warmest and most inspiring of companions. I hope this book will leave readers glad that they, too, know him a little.

ACKNOWLEDGEMENTS

Anyone who writes, or indeed reads, about Maxwell owes a great debt to Lewis Campbell, who gave us an affectionate yet penetrating picture of his lifelong friend in *The Life of James Clerk Maxwell*, co-written with William Garnett and published 3 years after Maxwell's death. Campbell and Garnett's book has been the principal source of information for all subsequent biographies and I would like to add my tribute and my thanks to those given by other authors.

I am also much indebted to the more recent biographers Francis Everitt, Ivan Tolstoy and Martin Goldman for their added insights, to Daniel Siegel and Peter Harman for their scholarly but reader-friendly analyses of Maxwell's work, and to the other authors listed in the bibliography. Several patient friends have kindly read drafts and suggested improvements; among these I am particularly grateful to Harold Allan and Bill Crouch. John Bilsland supplied excellent line drawings for the figures, and David Ritchie and Dick Dougal located many of the sources for the illustrations.

The Royal Societies of London and Edinburgh gave valuable help, as did the Royal Institution of Great Britain, King's College London, the University of Aberdeen, Trinity College Cambridge, the University of Cambridge Department of Physics, Cambridge University Library, the Institution of Civil Engineers, the Institution of Electrical Engineers and Clifton College.

A visit to Maxwell's birthplace at 14 India Street, Edinburgh, is a moving experience for anyone with an interest in Maxwell. It is possible only because the trustees of the James Clerk Maxwell Foundation service acquired the house in 1993 and have with trouble and care created a small but evocative museum. I should like to thank them for this service.

I am especially grateful to Sam Callander and to David and Astrid Ritchie for their generous encouragement and kindness.

The final words of thanks go to Wiley for publishing the book, and especially to my editor Sally Smith and her assistant Jill Jeffries for their friendly and expert help and guidance.

CHRONOLOGY

Principal events in Maxwell's life

1831 **Born at 14 India Street, Edinburgh, 13 June. Grew up at Glenlair**

1839 **His mother, Frances, died**

1841 **Started school, Edinburgh Academy**

1846 Published his first paper, on oval curves

1847 **Started at University of Edinburgh**

1848 Published paper *On Rolling Curves*

1850 Published paper *On the Equilibrium of Elastic Solids*

Started at Cambridge University, Peterhouse for one term, then Trinity

1854 **Finished undergraduate studies at Cambridge: second wrangler, joint winner of Smith's Prize: started post-graduate work**

1855 Published paper *Experiments on Colour as Perceived by the Eye*

Published first part of paper *On Faraday's Lines of Force*, second part the following year

Elected Fellow of Trinity

1856 **His father, John, died**

Appointed Professor of Natural Philosophy at Marischal College, Aberdeen

1858 Awarded Adams' Prize for essay *On the Stability of the Motion of Saturn's Rings*, paper published 1859

1858 **Married Katherine Mary Dewar, daughter of Principal of Marischal College**

1860 Published papers *Illustrations of the Dynamical Theory of Gases* and *On the Theory of Compound Colours and the Relations of the Colours of the Spectrum*

	Made redundant from Marischal College
	Failed in application for Chair of Natural Philosophy at University of Edinburgh
	Severely ill from smallpox
	Appointed Professor of Natural Philosophy at King's College, London
	Awarded Rumford Medal by the Royal Society of London for his work on colour vision
1861	Produced world's first colour photograph
	Published first two parts of paper *On Physical Lines of Force*, the remaining two parts the following year
	Elected FRS
1863	Published recommendations on electrical units and results of experiment to produce a standard of electrical resistance in his Committee's report to the British Association for the Advancement of Science
1865	Published paper *On Reciprocal Figures and Diagrams of Force*
	Published paper *A Dynamical Theory of the Electromagnetic Field*
	Severely ill from infection from cut sustained in riding accident
	Resigned chair at King's College London; returned to live at Glenlair
1866	Published paper *On the Viscosity or Internal Friction of Air and Other Gases*
1867	Published paper *On the Dynamical Theory of Gases*
	Visited Italy
1868	Published paper *On Governors*
	Carried out experiment to measure the ratio of the electrostatic and electromagnetic units of charge, which by his theory was equal to the speed of light
	Applied for but failed to get post of Principal of St Andrews University
1870	Published paper *On Hills and Dales*
	Awarded Keith Medal by the Royal Society of Edinburgh for work on reciprocal diagrams for engineering structures

1871 Published book *The Theory of Heat*, in which he introduced Maxwell's demon

Appointed Professor of Experimental Physics at Cambridge University

Supervised design and construction of Cavendish Laboratory building (fully operational 1874)

1873 Published book *A Treatise on Electricity and Magnetism*

1876 Published book *Matter and Motion*

1879 Published paper *On Boltzmann's Theorem on the Average Distribution of a Number of Material Points*

Published paper *On Stresses in Rarefied Gases Arising from Inequalities in Temperature*

Published book *Electrical Researches of the Honourable Henry Cavendish*

Died at Cambridge 5 November; buried at Parton

Note: Maxwell published five books and about 100 papers. Those of his writings that are described in the narrative are listed here and are available, with others, under titles listed in the Bibliography.

CAST OF CHARACTERS

Maxwell's relations and close friends

Blackburn, Hugh: Professor of Mathematics at Glasgow University, husband of Jemima.

Blackburn, Jemima (née Wedderburn): James' cousin, daughter of Isabella Wedderburn

Butler, Henry Montagu: student friend at Cambridge, afterwards Headmaster of Harrow School and, later, Master of Trinity College, Cambridge

Campbell, Lewis: schoolfriend, afterwards Professor of Greek at St Andrews University

Campbell, Robert: younger brother of Lewis

Cay, Charles Hope: James' cousin, son of Robert

Cay, Jane: James' aunt, younger sister of Frances Clerk Maxwell

Cay, John: James' uncle, elder brother of Frances Clerk Maxwell

Cay, Robert: James' uncle, younger brother of Frances Clerk Maxwell

Cay, William Dyce: James' cousin, son of Robert

Clerk, Sir George: James' uncle, elder brother of John Clerk Maxwell

Clerk Maxwell, Frances (née Cay): James' mother

Clerk Maxwell, John: James' father

Clerk Maxwell, Katherine Mary (née Dewar): James' wife

Dewar, Daniel: James' father-in-law, Principal of Marischal College, Aberdeen

Dunn, Elizabeth (Lizzie) (née Cay): James' cousin, daughter of Robert Cay

Forbes, James: friend and mentor, Professor of Natural Philosophy at Edinburgh University, afterwards Principal of St Andrew's University

Hort, Fenton John Anthony: student friend at Cambridge, afterwards a professor at Cambridge

Litchfield, Richard Buckley: student friend at Cambridge, afterwards Secretary of the London Working Men's College

Mackenzie, Colin: James' cousin once removed, son of Janet Mackenzie

Mackenzie, Janet (née Wedderburn): James' cousin, daughter of Isabella Wedderburn

Monro, Cecil James: student friend at Cambridge, afterwards a frequent correspondent with James, particularly on colour vision

Pomeroy, Robert Henry: student friend at Cambridge who joined the Indian Civil Service and died in his 20s during the Indian Mutiny

Tait, Peter Guthrie: schoolfriend, afterwards Professor of Natural Philosophy at Edinburgh University

Thomson, William, later Baron Kelvin of Largs: friend (and mentor in early stages of James' career), Professor of Natural Philosophy at Glasgow University

Wedderburn, Isabella (née Clerk): James' aunt, younger sister of John Clerk Maxwell

Wedderburn, James: James' uncle by marriage, husband of Isabella

Note: The list shows those of Maxwell's relations and close friends who are mentioned in the narrative, and two more who are included to explain relationships. His work colleagues and associates are not listed here, apart from Forbes, Tait and Thomson.

INTRODUCTION

One scientific epoch ended and another began with James Clerk Maxwell

Albert Einstein

From a long view of the history of mankind—seen from, say, ten thousand years from now—there can be little doubt that the most significant event of the nineteenth century will be judged as Maxwell's discovery of the laws of electrodynamics.

Richard Feynmann

In 1861, James Clerk Maxwell had a scientific idea that was as profound as any work of philosophy, as beautiful as any painting, and more powerful than any act of politics or war. Nothing would be the same again.

In the middle of the nineteenth century the world's best physicists had been searching long and hard for a key to the great mystery of electricity and magnetism. The two phenomena seemed to be inextricably linked but the ultimate nature of the linkage was subtle and obscure, defying all attempts to winkle it out. Then Maxwell found the answer with as pure a shaft of genius as has ever been seen.

He made the astounding prediction that fleeting electric currents could exist not only in conductors but in all materials, and even in empty space. Here was the missing part of the linkage; now everything fitted into a complete and beautiful theory of electromagnetism.

This was not all. The theory predicted that every time a magnet jiggled, or an electric current changed, a wave of energy would spread out into space like a ripple on a pond. Maxwell calculated the speed of the waves and it turned out to be the very speed at which light had been measured. At a stroke, he had united electricity, magnetism and light. Moreover, visible light was only a small band in a vast range of possible waves, which all travelled at the same speed but vibrated at different frequencies.

Maxwell's ideas were so different from anything that had gone before that most of his contemporaries were bemused; even some admirers thought he was indulging in a wild fantasy. No proof came until a quarter of a century later, when Heinrich Hertz produced waves from a spark-gap source and detected them.

Over the past 100 years we have learnt to use Maxwell's waves to send information over great and small distances in tiny fractions of a second. Today we can scarcely imagine a world without radio, television and radar. His brainchild has changed our lives profoundly and irrevocably.

Maxwell's theory is now an established law of nature, one of the central pillars of our understanding of the universe. It opened the way to the two great triumphs of twentieth century physics, relativity and quantum theory, and survived both of those violent revolutions completely intact. As another great physicist, Max Planck, put it, the theory must be numbered among the greatest of all intellectual achievements. But its results are now so closely woven into the fabric of our daily lives that most of us take it wholly for granted, its author unacknowledged.

What makes the situation still more poignant is that Maxwell would be among the world's greatest scientists even if he had never set to work on electricity and magnetism. His influence is everywhere. He introduced statistical methods into physics; now they are used as a matter of course. He demonstrated the principle by which we see colours and took the world's first colour photograph. His whimsical creation, *Maxwell's demon*—a molecule-sized creature who could make heat flow from a cold gas to a hot one—was the first effective scientific thought experiment, a technique Einstein later made his own. It posed questions that perplexed scientists for 60 years and stimulated the creation of information theory, which underpins our communications and computing. He wrote a paper on automatic control systems many

years before anyone else gave thought to the subject; it became the foundation of modern control theory and cybernetics. He designed the Cavendish Laboratory and, as its founding Director, started a brilliant revival of Cambridge's scientific tradition which led on to the discoveries of the electron and the structure of DNA.

Some of his work gave direct practical help to engineers. He showed how to use polarised light to reveal strain patterns in a structure and invented a neat and powerful graphical method for calculating the forces in any framework; both techniques became standard engineering practice. He was also the first to suggest using a centrifuge to separate gases.

Maxwell was born in 1831 and lived for 48 years. A native Scotsman, he spent about half of his working life in England. From his earliest days he was fascinated by the world and determined to find out how it worked. Like all parents, his were assailed with questions, but to be interrogated by 3 year-old James must have been an experience of a different order. Everything that moved, shone or made a noise drew the question 'What's the go o' that?' and, if he was not satisfied, the follow-up 'but what's the *particular* go of it?'. A casual comment about a blue stone brought the response 'but how d'ye *know* it's blue?'. Maxwell's childish curiosity stayed with him and he spent most of his adult life trying to work out the 'go' of things. At the task of unravelling nature's deep secrets he was supreme.

Those in the know honour Maxwell alongside Newton and Einstein, yet most of us have never heard of him. This is an injustice and a mystery but most of all it is our own great loss. One excellent reason for telling this story is to try to gain Maxwell a little of the public recognition he so clearly deserves, but a much better one is to try to make good the loss. His was a life for all of us to enjoy. He was not only a consummate scientist but a man of extraordinary personal charm and generous spirit: inspiring, entertaining and entirely without vanity. His friends loved and admired him in equal measure and felt better for knowing him. Perhaps we can share a tiny part of that experience.

CHAPTER ONE

A COUNTRY BOY

Glenlair 1831–1841

When they had their first glimpse of the newcomer, the boys of the second year class could scarcely contain their hostile curiosity. He was wearing an absurd loose tweed tunic with a frilly collar and curious square-toed shoes with brass buckles, the like of which had never been seen at the Edinburgh Academy. At the first break between lessons they swarmed around the new boy, baiting him unmercifully, and when he answered their taunts in a strange Galloway accent they let out whoops of jubilant derision. At the end of a long day he arrived home with clothes in tatters. He seemed to be dull in class and soon acquired the nickname 'Dafty'. The rough treatment went on, yet he bore it all with remarkable good humour until one day, when provoked beyond endurance, he turned on his tormentors with a ferocity that astonished them. They showed him more respect after that, but the name 'Dafty' stuck. So started the academic career of one of the greatest scientists of all time, James Clerk Maxwell.

The first 8 years of his life had been wonderfully happy. He was born in Edinburgh[1] but brought up at Glenlair, his father's estate in the gently rolling Vale of Urr in the Galloway region of south-west Scotland[2]. His parents, John and Frances Clerk Maxwell, had married late and their first child, Elizabeth, had died in infancy. Frances was almost 40 when James was born. She and John adored their son and watched over his development with indulgent devotion. As soon as he could walk and talk a little it became plain that he was a remarkable boy. Like all children he was curious about everything around him, but his curiosity was of a different order and reached into places rarely explored. For example, it was not enough for him to discover how to ring the house bells; he had to find out which of the bell-pulls around the house rang which bell in the kitchen and where all the wires ran. And he could turn everyday objects to surprising uses. One day his nurse Maggy gave him a tin plate to play with. Perhaps he first tried banging it with a spoon or rolling it across the floor but soon he was excitedly calling his mother and father to come and see how he had brought the sun into the house by reflecting its image off the plate on to a wall.

As he grew, he played rough-and-tumble games with the local children, climbed trees, explored the fields and woods and watched the animals and birds with rapt attention. He enjoyed the morning chore of fetching water from the river by cart. Nothing that went on in the house escaped his attention. Nobody could do anything without having young James appear, demanding a full explanation and insisting on having a go himself. He knitted, made baskets, took a hand in the baking and helped his father design and plan improvements to the estate. Like all boys he could be a little monkey at times. One evening, just after dark, he blew out the candle as Maggy was approaching with the tea tray and lay down in the doorway.

He quickly learnt to read and, under his mother's guidance, began to understand the wider world. He enjoyed history and geography and, especially, literature. Before long he was reading everything within reach. Milton and Shakespeare were particular favourites. What is more, he seemed to remember most of what he had read.

For entertainment, the family would often read novels or poetry aloud or act out a play. And religion was an important part of the domestic routine: every day the household, including servants, met for prayers and every Sunday they went to Parton church, five miles to the west. His father's background was

Presbyterian, his mother's Episcopalian, but both took a tolerant view of doctrinal matters. The Clerk Maxwells played their full part in the social life of the area; there were fairs and dances and visits exchanged with other leading families. There were also visits to and from relations in Edinburgh and Penicuik, the estate of James' uncle.

Life at Glenlair was harmonious, stimulating and gently bustling. It was also full of jokes and banter. There was no pomposity whatever—no person, institution or topic was above some gentle debunking. The spirit of these times stayed with James all his life. We shall see this demonstrated time and again but, even so, let us cheat a little by taking a glimpse now at a poem he wrote when he was 26, teasing his friend William Thomson, who was consultant to the Atlantic Telegraph Company, when its cable-laying ran into difficulties.

> Under the sea, under the sea,
> No little signals are coming to me.
> Under the sea, under the sea,
> Something has surely gone wrong,
> And it's broke, broke, broke;
> What is the cause of it does not transpire
> But something has broken the telegraph wire
> With a stroke, stroke, stroke,
> Or else they've been pulling too strong.[3]

No *Schadenfreude* here. Maxwell admired the transatlantic cable project immensely and even suggested how they might lay the cable more smoothly and economically by using an underwater kite. He just couldn't resist poking a little fun.

James' parents were fairly new arrivals in the Happy Valley, as the Vale of Urr was known to its residents. John Clerk Maxwell was an advocate who had lived most of his life in Edinburgh. He had an adequate private income and it did not matter much to him that his practice never flourished. John's heart lay elsewhere —in his hobby, which was what we would now call technology. He had built up a wide range of friends in industry, agriculture and universities and enjoyed keeping abreast of new ideas. His life ticked away pleasantly but ineffectively until events took a turn when he was in his late 30s. A long-standing acquaintance with the sister of a friend blossomed into romance and she agreed to marry him. Frances Cay was a spirited and resolute woman who supplied the get-up-and-go he had so far lacked. Both their lives were transformed and Glenlair was the focus. John had inherited the estate some years before and had toyed with the idea of going to live there and applying his ideas on farming. Now the day-dreams changed into hard and purposeful activity—they resolved on setting up home at Glenlair.

Previous owners of the estate had been absentee landlords and there was no suitable dwelling there. But to John this was an advantage: the prospect of designing and building his own family house was irresistible. The house he designed was a modest one for a country gentleman of that time—he planned to extend it later. Impatient to start their new life, he and Frances moved to Glenlair soon after building started and lived in one of the estate cottages until the house was habitable. They launched themselves wholeheartedly into country life, then endured the anguish when their first child died. When Frances became pregnant for the second time they decided to go to Edinburgh for the birth, to be near relations and hospital if needed. Soon after James was born they returned home and family life began.

Glenlair had belonged to John's family for only three generations. It was the 1500 acre residue of a much larger estate called Middlebie, which had been the seat of the fierce Maxwell clan. John's family name was Clerk: by the normal reckoning he was not really a Maxwell at all; neither was James. The Clerks had acquired the Middlebie estate by marriage in addition to their own baronetcy of Penicuik, 10 miles south of Edinburgh. They arranged that Penicuik would be passed on to the senior heir and Middlebie to the second, and that whoever inherited Middlebie would add Maxwell to the family name. When John's grandfather lost a fortune in mining investments most of Middlebie had to be sold, leaving only Glenlair. So it came about that James' father was John Clerk Maxwell of Glenlair while his uncle was Sir George Clerk of Penicuik.

John and Frances came from exceptionally talented families—previous generations of Clerks and Cays had distinguished themselves in many fields[4]. To do justice to this point would take us too far from our story, but two examples from the Clerk line will give an idea.

James' great-great-grandfather, Sir John Clerk, was the kind of man whose easy brilliance at everything he did makes most of us despair of our own efforts. As well as being a Baron of the Exchequer of Scotland and a Commissioner of the Union he wrote good music that is still performed today. He was a Fellow of the Royal Society and an influential authority in archaeology, architecture, history, astronomy, geology and medicine.

One of Sir John's sons, another John Clerk, was a spectacularly successful businessman as well as a gifted artist and geologist. He worked with his friend James Hutton and illustrated a volume of Hutton's seminal work, *Theory of the Earth*. But his masterpiece was an essay on naval tactics. It is extraordinary that a landlubber—he never went to sea—should even think of writing such a book, but what is more remarkable is that it became the standard work on the subject. Nelson used several sentences straight from the essay in his orders for the battle of Trafalgar.

There was little evidence in John and Frances' homely house at Glenlair of their illustrious antecedents. No grand family silver, no portrait gallery. Their one prized heirloom was a battered set of bagpipes which James' grandfather, a captain in the British East India Company's Navy, had used to keep afloat when he was shipwrecked. The lack of formal trappings made it a wonderful home for their son. James had a much closer relationship with his parents than was usual among the gentry; his mother became his tutor and his father often took him along when dealing with estate business. This still left him plenty of time to run around with the local children. He learnt their Galloway speech and acquired a local accent that he would never entirely lose. No child could have been happier, but sadness was to come.

Frances became ill and abdominal cancer was diagnosed. She decided to have an operation without anaesthetic. The chances of success were slim but she wanted to live longer if possible for the sake of her husband and son and so chose to undergo this excruciating treatment. But the operation was not successful and Frances died soon afterwards. She was 47 years old.

Frances had been the hub of the family; without her the house at Glenlair must have been a desolate place for a while. Heavy of heart, John and James were glad, at least, that her suffering was over. The loss brought them even closer together and the father enjoyed his son's lively companionship. There was, however, the problem of schooling. The plan had been for James to be educated at home until he was 13, when he would go straight to university. But John was too busy with the estate and with various county boards and committees to teach the boy himself. There was no suitable school within daily travelling distance and he dreaded the loneliness that would follow if he sent James away.

He decided to engage a private tutor and chose a 16 year-old boy from the neighbourhood. The lad had done well in exams at school but delayed going to university so he could take the post. No-one then or since has been able to fathom how John Clerk Maxwell came to make such an ill-judged choice. Knowing he had an exceptionally gifted son, how could he entrust his education to a youth with little knowledge and no experience of life beyond school? Whatever the reasons, the results were disastrous.

The tutor used the methods by which he had himself been taught: rote learning encouraged by physical chastisement. The lessons became a moral and physical ordeal. James wanted to please his father but saw no sense in the mechanical recitation of words and numbers divorced from any meaning. No amount of ear pulling and cuffing about the head could persuade him to learn in that fashion. His local friends had no doubt suffered similar treatment at school, so perhaps he thought it was simply something that had to be endured. But eventually, after more than a year of torment, he rebelled.

Beside a duck pond near the house was a large washtub that James used to use as an improvised boat. In the middle of a lesson, his tolerance exhausted, he ran out, pushed the tub into the water, jumped in and paddled himself to the deepest part of the pond. Ignoring the tutor's urgings, he refused to come in. Although reproved by his father for this act of rebellion, James had made his point.

His Aunt Jane, Frances' younger sister, who lived in Edinburgh, was quick to understand what had been going on and persuaded John that it was high time that 10 year-old James had proper schooling. John's widowed sister, James' Aunt Isabella, who also lived in Edinburgh, agreed. The Edinburgh Academy[5], one of the best schools in Scotland, was only a short walk from her house; James could stay with her during term time and return to Glenlair for the holidays. Much as he hated the thought of parting from his son, John could see that Jane and Isabella were right and agreed to the plan.

Unfortunately, the first year class was full, so James had to enrol in the second. There he would be joining a class of 60 older boys who had already spent more than a year in the school, long enough to have absorbed its conventions and developed their own schoolboy culture. They were mostly from smart Edinburgh families and spoke with refined accents. Clearly, life was not going to be easy for the newcomer. What made things even harder was that his father had designed and made special clothes for him. From a logical standpoint, they were excellent: warm, hard-wearing and comfortable, with a loose tunic and square-toed shoes. But John seemed oblivious to the human factor: to the boys in James' new class, in their conventional tight jackets and slim shoes, the newcomer looked like a ridiculous peasant from a foreign land.

So it was that James arrived for his first day at the city school, a country boy with a strange accent and wearing peculiar clothes. As we have seen, he was tough enough to ride out his rough reception and parry the taunts. A hard time lay ahead, but in the end the attitude of his classmates was to turn from ridicule to acceptance, and finally to admiration.

CHAPTER TWO

PINS AND STRING

Edinburgh Academy 1841–1847

Aunt Isabella and Aunt Jane promptly saw to it that James was kitted out in the same style as the other boys, but he did not think or behave like them. He rarely joined in formal sports and, although he enjoyed playground games with marbles and tops, he still insisted on calling them 'bools' and 'pearies' as he had done at Glenlair. He brought along crude mechanical contraptions and drew curious diagrams but none of his fellows could make head or tail of them. Often he went alone to a corner of the play area which had some trees and a grassy bank where he watched the bees and beetles or improvised gymnastic exercises on the branches.

His mind was a-whirr with impressions, thoughts and part-formed ideas. For a long while these found no expression at school. He was, as a classmate later put it, like a locomotive under full steam but with the wheels not gripping the track. More than a year went by before he made a real friend. But he showed himself to be strong and brave and these qualities commanded respect. He sought no quarrels and bore no grudges: for all his odd ways it became plain to everyone that he was good-natured and generous.

Two things held him back in class at first. One was the numbing effect of the repetitive exercises in Greek and Latin, harking back to the time with his tutor. The other was a hesitancy of speech, the words coming in spates between long pauses. This defect remained with him to some extent all his life and may also have stemmed from his time under the tutor. He eventually managed to overcome the worst of the problem by projecting a mental image of answers to the master's anticipated questions on to the classroom windows, so he could simply read them out when needed.

At Aunt Isabella's house[1] there were no such problems. Life there was congenial and stimulating. The library was even better stocked than that at Glenlair and he was soon reading Swift and Dryden.

He loved to draw and had the example of his cousin Jemima, who had often brought her sketchbook to Glenlair and was now a rising young artist. Landseer had said that 'in portraying animals he had nothing to teach her' and she was soon to have pictures exhibited in the Royal Academy[2]. Jemima was also learning woodcutting and let James borrow her tools. His artistic efforts displayed more gusto than skill but had a rugged charm that made them his own.

Sometimes he and Jemima combined their talents by producing 'wheels of life' for parlour entertainment. A series of pictures, like an animated cartoon film, was set on a spinning wheel or cylinder so that one saw the images in rapid succession and got the impression of movement. James designed and made the machines and sketched sequences of pictures, which Jemima would then draw—a favourite sequence showed a rider doing acrobatic tricks on the back of a galloping horse.

His father came to Edinburgh whenever he could. When he was in town on a Saturday the two would walk up the rocky hill, Arthur's Seat, or visit other local attractions. Every new experience fed James' probing and retentive mind. One of these Saturday treats was to see an exhibition of 'electromagnetic machines'. The sight of these primitive devices—nothing like the generators and motors we know today—started in the boy's mind a process of thought that would ultimately transform the way physicists think about the world, a change that Einstein called 'the most profound and useful that physics has experienced since the time of Newton'.

When they were apart, father and son wrote to one another frequently. James' letters were full of childish jokes in which his father clearly took delight. He signed them with anagrams of his name, such as Jas Alex McMerkwell, and addressed some of them to Mr John Clerk Maxwell, Postyknowswhere, Kirkpatrick Durham, Dumfries. One letter, just after his 13th birthday, gives a tiny hint of things to come. After fulsome accounts of a minstrel show and a trip to the beach, he asks about events and people at Glenlair and finally mentions 'I have made a tetrahedron and a dodecahedron and two more hedrons that I don't know the right names for'. He had not yet learnt any geometry in school but had somehow found out about what mathematicians call the regular polyhedra: solid figures whose faces are all identical polygons and whose vertex angles are all equal. There are only five of them: the most familiar is the cube, which has six faces; the others have four, eight, 12 and 20. James quickly worked out how to make them out of pasteboard and went on to make other symmetrical solids derived from the basic ones.

We do not know what triggered his thoughts on this topic: he may have read something but it is unlikely to have been a mathematical account. Whatever the stimulus, James' response showed an intuitive grasp of symmetry and a flair for exploring different forms of it, qualities that later shone through his scientific work.

At first, the method of teaching in James' class was not very different from that of his old tutor. The boys spent long hours reciting Greek verbs and doing routine arithmetical exercises, and the class master, Mr Carmichael, was free with the tawse —a fearsome leather strap cut into strips at the end. But gradually the rote-based drudgery gave way to more appealing work and James began to take interest and be noticed. From somewhere near the bottom of the class in his first year, he rose to 19th overall in the second and won the prize for scripture biography.

He came to see that Greek and Latin were worth learning and his position in class improved. As the boys had to sit in places corresponding to their rank in the class, he now found himself in more sympathetic company. His knowledge of the Bible, which probably exceeded that of the masters, helped him to win the scripture biography prize in his second year, but it was in the third year that things really started to happen. Mathematics lessons began and 'Dafty' astonished his classmates by the ease and speed with which he mastered geometry. His confidence boosted, he became less reticent in the other lessons; he began to shine in English and was soon in the top group in all subjects.

By a stroke of luck, Lewis Campbell's family moved to a house almost next door to Aunt Isabella's. Lewis was the star of James' class, a very clever boy who was well liked and usually came top. He and James had just begun to strike up a friendship before the move. Now they walked home together, often continuing the conversation by an open front door until voices from inside complained of the draught. The world opened up for James. For the first time he could share his teeming ideas with someone of his own age. Geometry was their first common ground but soon the topics ranged over the full sweep of their experiences and thoughts. It became a lifelong friendship. When Maxwell died at the age of 48, Campbell wrote a moving biography.

James' friendship with Lewis Campbell put an end to his social isolation in school. Soon he found himself among a group of boys with lively minds who enjoyed his whimsical chatter and his unending flow of thought-provoking ideas. Among them was another who was to become a lifelong friend, Peter Guthrie Tait[3].

P. G. Tait became one of Scotland's finest physicists. As we shall see, the careers of Maxwell and Tait ran closely in parallel: more than once they found themselves competing for the same post. But friendship far outstripped rivalry and they continued the practice, begun as schoolboys, of bouncing ideas off one another. At school the two of them were always challenging each other with 'props', mathematical propositions or problems[4]. One was to find the shape of a mirror that would show a person his image the right way round. When both were senior professors, their letters, or more often postcards, were still written in a kind of schoolboy argot, more polished than that of 25 years earlier but just as exuberant.

We now come to James' first publication. He was 14. It was about the kinds of curves that can be drawn on a piece of paper using pins, string and a pencil. Everyone knows that if you (1) stick in a pin, (2) tie one end of a piece of string to it and the other end to a pencil and (3) draw a curve by moving the pencil with the string taut, then the curve will be a circle. Groundsmen use the same method to mark out the circles in the middle of football pitches. People who have studied a little geometry will know that the construction can be modified in an interesting way. If you use two pins instead of one, tie one end of the string to each, push the pencil against the string and move the pencil while keeping the string taut, you get an oval-shaped curve called an ellipse. Each pin is at one of the two focal points of the ellipse (just as the sun is at one focal point of the earth's elliptical orbit). If you put the pins close together the ellipse will be almost like a circle; the further you put them apart, the flatter the oval shape becomes.

For most people this would be the end of the matter. Not so for James. He untied one end of the string from its pin and tied it to the pencil instead. Then he looped the string around the free pin, pushed the pencil against it to make it taut, and drew another curve. It was a pleasing but lop-sided oval, like the outline of an egg. This was just the beginning. He reasoned that the simple ellipse could be defined as the locus of a movable point from which the sum of the distances to the two focal points (pins) was constant (the length of the string). As an equation:

$$p + q = s$$

where p is the distance to one focal point, q is the distance to the other and s is the length of the string. When drawing his new oval he had doubled the string between the pencil and one of the two focal points, so the equation was:

$$2p + q = s$$

He drew more curves, varying the number of times he looped the string around each pin, and got various egg-shaped ovals with different degrees of pointedness. He saw that, in principle, he could loop the string any number of times around either pin and thus generate a whole family of ovals:

$$mp + nq = s$$

where m and n are any integers. He then went on to draw curves with three, four and five focal points.

It was not unusual for James to produce geometrical propositions. He was doing it all the time. But his father decided to show this set to James Forbes, a friend who was professor of natural philosophy at Edinburgh University. He and his mathematical colleague Philip Kelland were struck by the boy's ingenuity.

They combed the mathematical archives to see if anything at all similar had been done before. Sure enough, it had—by no less a person than René Descartes, the famous seventeenth century French mathematician and philosopher. Descartes had discovered the same set of bi-focal ovals but James' results were more general and his construction method simpler. What is more, his equation for bi-focal curves turned out to have a practical application in optics.

Here was James' debut on the scientific stage. Forbes read the paper[5] to the Royal Society of Edinburgh because James was deemed too young to do it himself. It generated a lot of interest. Among those interested was D. R. Hay, a printer and an artist whose attempts to create pleasing shapes by mathematical means were well known in Edinburgh. It was his quest for 'the perfect oval' that had prompted James to experiment with pins and string. It transpired that Hay had also tried pins and string and had eventually had some success using three pins. But he used just a simple loop. This gave an oval made up from three part-ellipses joined together, neat but not very beautiful. The question 'Why didn't I think of that?' comes to all of us at some time but rarely as emphatically as it must have struck Mr Hay when he saw James' solution.

Level-headed as he was, James enjoyed the celebrity. His father was pleased as Punch. But the ovals paper marked the start of James' scientific career in another, far more significant, way. It introduced him to the work of René Descartes, one of the great creators of mathematics. As it happens, he soon found a small mistake in the great man's calculations, but the overwhelming feeling he had was one of fellowship. He went on in later years to read the work of all the pioneers in each area of science to which he turned his hand.

The great men became his friends; he appreciated their struggles, knowing that most discoveries come only after a period of stumbling and fumbling. By also studying philosophy he gained a deeper insight into the *processes* of scientific discovery than any other man of his time. Nobody understood better than Maxwell the broad sweep of historical development in science. Set alongside this knowledge was his own extraordinary originality and intuition. Together, these components produced what the great American physicist Robert Millikan described as 'one of the most penetrating intellects of all time'.

One of the things Maxwell learned from his reading was the fallibility of men's efforts to understand the world. All of the great scientists had made mistakes. He was acutely aware of his own tendency to make errors in calculation. 'I am quite capable of writing a fancy formula', he once wrote to a friend, meaning a wrong formula. In fact, his intuition often led him to correct results even when he had made mistakes along the way. When reading the work of fellow scientists, past or present, he was tolerant of mistakes but sharply critical of any failure to be honest and open with the reader. Poisson is rebuked for 'telling lies about the way people make barometers' and Ampère for describing only polished demonstrations of his law of the force between wires carrying electric currents and hiding the rougher experiments by which he had originally discovered the law.

James enjoyed his last 2 years in school despite several periods of sickness: although strong and athletic he was prone to spells of ill-health. His achievements in English matched those in mathematics: he seemed to have no trouble recalling anything he had read and showed an amazing facility for composing verse on any topic in impeccable rhyme and metre. He also won school prizes for history, geography and French, and came second overall in his class in the final year. He entertained his fellows with whimsical poems and discussed all manner of things with Lewis Campbell, P. G. Tait and other boys with a serious turn of mind. One of them later recalled how the school governors, no doubt wishing to impress parents of future pupils, decided to add the new subject of 'physical science' to the curriculum without too much concern over who would teach it. All he could remember of the lessons was that Maxwell and Tait knew a lot more than the master did.

Sometimes James would stay for a while in his Aunt Jane's house in a nearby part of the town[6]. As his mother's sister, and with no children of her own, Aunt Jane did her best to give the boy the sort of guidance she felt Frances would have done. Kind-hearted but sharp of tongue, she could have been a character model for David Copperfield's Aunt, Betsy Trotwood. She tried to soften James' eccentricities and improve his social poise: when his thoughts were distracted by the pattern of light in a table glass or the swaying of a candle flame he would be recalled to the company by a sharp 'Jamesie, you're in a prop'.

She also saw to it that he attended the Episcopal church every Sunday as well as the Presbyterian one, and arranged for him to go to her friend Dean Ramsay's catechism classes. Ramsay was good with young people and used to caution them against being carried away by the breakaway Presbyterian Free Church movement or any of the zealous new religious groups. In fact, James needed no such warning. His faith was the guiding principle of his life but it was an intensely reflective personal faith which could not be contained within the rules of a sect. Institutional politics, whether of the church, the state or the university, was a topic that never engaged his interest.

Another favourite relation was Uncle John. John Cay was his mother's and Aunt Jane's elder brother, and his father's long-standing friend. Like John Clerk Maxwell he was a lawyer, but a more successful one who became a judge. The two Johns shared an enthusiasm for technology. In their younger days they had tried without success to make and market useful inventions; one project was for a bellows that would produce a continuous, even blast. One day he took James and Lewis Campbell to visit William Nicol, the celebrated experimental optician, who had invented a way of polarising light using prisms made from carefully cut Iceland spar. Prisms like these later became known simply as nicols, part of the standard toolkit. James was fascinated by all he saw in Nicol's workshop and the visit was to have an important sequel.

The best times of all were holidays at Glenlair. James kept up his local friendships and joined in the Happy Valley social life. There was riding, walking the hills, picnics and archery in the summer, and curling in the winter. He helped the farm workers bring in the harvest. The one pastime James avoided was shooting. He did not condemn others; it was simply that he could not bring himself to do it. He loved animals of all kinds and seemed to have an easy rapport with them: he could ride the most wilful horse and teach any dog to do tricks.

He made himself useful by helping his father with estate business. The property had been in a poor state when his parents moved there. The building of the house had taken up most of what John could afford and the rest had to go into basic land improvements like stone clearance, drainage and fencing. Gradually, more was done and John was able to put up the outbuildings he had planned from the start. Plans to extend the house and replace the ford across the river Urr by a bridge still had to wait.

Not all holidays were taken at Glenlair. Christmases were generally spent with James' uncle Sir George Clerk at Penicuik, where skating was a big attraction. After a busy political career, Sir George was at this time Master of the Royal Mint. He was also an accomplished amateur zoologist who later became President of the Zoological Society. His political skills were needed there; two of his Vice Presidents were renowned swashbucklers who held opposing views on just about everything. Their most famous clash was at a meeting at Oxford in 1860, where Bishop 'Soapy Sam' Wilberforce set out to smash Darwin's theory of the Origin of Species but was himself demolished by Thomas Henry Huxley.

There were visits to Glasgow to see James' cousin Jemima, who was by now living there. She had fallen in love with and married Hugh Blackburn, Professor of Mathematics at Glasgow University. Hugh was friendly with the ebullient new Professor of Natural Philosophy, William Thomson. Appointed professor at the age of 22, Thomson was a brilliant and inspirational man. In the course of 53 years in the same post he became, as Lord Kelvin, the patriarch of British science. He could see at once that the boy had a rare gift and the two struck up a friendship which lasted throughout Maxwell's life. Thomson was a man from whom ideas flew like sparks. He and Faraday were the two people whose work most influenced Maxwell's own.

Every minute of James' day was occupied. When on his own at home he would read, write letters, work at his 'props', or try experiments in an improvised laboratory. His only frivolous diversion was to practise tricks with the devil on two sticks*—a kind of top which could be spun, thrown and caught using a string tied to two hand-held sticks—on which he soon became a virtuoso. Even then he was no doubt sharpening his insight into the theory of angular momentum.

Given what we have seen of his life so far, one would have thought there could be no doubt that he would take up science as a career. But his father wanted him to go in for the law. To understand why, we must try to picture the situation.

In mid nineteenth century Britain the word 'scientist' had not yet come into common use. Physicists and chemists called themselves 'natural philosophers' and biologists called themselves 'natural historians'. Many people who did scientific work were gentlemen of independent means. Others were clergymen or

* The game later became widely known under the name 'diabolo'.

doctors or lawyers or businessmen for whom science was a hobby. Several members of the Clerk and Cay families were just such men. There were a few professional posts, in universities and in organisations like the Royal Observatory and the Royal Institution, but they were poorly paid and rarely became vacant because their holders tended to remain for life. Competition for the best posts was very stiff. Science was thought of as interesting but not particularly useful. There had been rapid advances in industry and transport but these had mostly been brought about by practical engineers with little formal scientific background. The problem of finding longitude at sea had been solved not by the mathematical astronomers but by John Harrison and his clocks. Some ingenious physicists, like Charles Wheatstone and William Thomson, were turning their talents to inventing devices for the new telegraph but, with this exception, little of the work of Faraday and others on electricity and magnetism had yet fed through to practical application. In short, science was a splendid hobby for a gentleman but a poor profession.

John may also have reflected on his own failure as an advocate and hoped that his son would make amends. James felt the tension between his father's wish and his own bent for science. But he was interested in plenty else besides: literature and philosophy were stimulating and, who knows, the law might draw him too when he got to know it.

In any case no decision had to be made yet. The next step was to enrol at Edinburgh University, where he would study mathematics under Philip Kelland, natural philosophy under James Forbes and logic under the famous Sir William Hamilton. James was looking forward to spreading his wings. He celebrated the move in characteristic fashion with a poem: an affectionately ironic tribute to his old school[7].

If ony here has got an ear,
  He'd better tak' a haud o' me
Or I'll begin, wi' roarin' din,
  To cheer our old Academy.

Dear old Academy,
Queer old Academy,
A merry lot were we, I wot,
When at the old Academy.

There's some may think me crouse wi' drink,
And some may think it mad o' me,
But ither some will gladly come
And cheer our old Academy.

Some set their hopes on Kings and Popes,
But o' the sons o' Adam, he
Was first, without the smallest doubt,
That built the first Academy.

Let pedants seek for scraps of Greek,
Their lingo to Macadamize;
Gie me the sense, without pretence,
That comes o' Scots Academies.

Let scholars all, both grit and small,
Of learning mourn the sad demise;
That's as they think, but we will drink
Good luck to Scots Academies.

CHAPTER THREE

PHILOSOPHY

Edinburgh University 1847–1850

James came to Edinburgh University at 16, a boy who had a penchant for science and mathematics but who would probably nevertheless follow his father's wish and go in for the law. He left for Cambridge University at 19 as a young man set on a scientific career.

The change of direction was urged on James' father by Hugh Blackburn and James Forbes as it became more and more clear that the boy's vocation was, in his own words, for 'another kind of laws'. John Clerk Maxwell was always slow to make up his mind but in the end made the right decision, as no doubt everyone knew he would. Cambridge was acknowledged to be the best university for anyone likely to make his mark in science and most writers about Maxwell express regret that he did not go there sooner. They may be right but, as we shall see, the 3 years at Edinburgh did much to make him the kind of scientist he was.

Scottish universities strove to open up higher education so that the 'lad o' pairts' from a humble background could take his place alongside the sons of gentlemen. They prided themselves on producing self-confident young men who would be able to tackle any task and hold their own in any company. The courses were broad: future doctors, lawyers, church ministers, teachers and engineers would study Latin, Greek, civil and natural history, mathematics, natural philosophy and mental philosophy. Mental philosophy—we would now call it simply philosophy—was the bedrock. At Edinburgh it carried more prestige than any other subject and had two professorships, one in logic and metaphysics and another in moral philosophy.

Faced with the choice of classes, James was like a hungry child in a cake shop. He decided to start with natural philosophy, mathematics and logic. At first the lectures in natural philosophy and mathematics were too elementary to be interesting but he was captivated at once by Sir William Hamilton's talks on logic, which soon spilled over to metaphysics and other aspects of philosophy. Hamilton—not to be confused with the Irish mathematician Sir William Rowan Hamilton—was a celebrated philosopher in his own right and an inspirational teacher. James had found someone who did not shirk from answering his awkward questions and he was delighted to find that the answers sometimes came in the form of yet deeper questions. There is little doubt that the profoundly philosophical approach which was to serve Maxwell so well in his work had its roots in Hamilton's classes.

To understand what this philosophical approach was, and why it was so important, we must take a short historical diversion. David Hume, the great eighteenth century Scottish philosopher, had put the cat among the pigeons with his notion of scepticism: that nothing can be proved, except in mathematics, and that much of what we take to be fact is merely conjecture. This alarmed some of his hard-headed countrymen, who reacted by starting their own 'Common Sense' school. They thought it was daft to doubt whether the world exists and wrong to doubt whether God exists. But, these things given, they rejected any belief or method that did not proceed directly from observed fact. The way to make scientific progress, they said, was by simple accretion of experimental results, a narrow interpretation of the principle of induction that the Englishman Francis Bacon had advocated more than a century earlier. Imagination had no place in their system.

In fact, the Common Sense school could hardly have been more wrong; empirical evidence is vital but all innovative scientists are

strongly imaginative and make full use of working hypotheses which are often drawn by analogy with other branches of science. Luckily the school's adherents eventually realised this and came to a view that truly *was* common sense: analogies and imaginative hypotheses can be wonderful but should be kept in their place; a scientist should remain sceptical about his own pet fancies even when they have led to progress. Many scientists cease to be creative when they fail this test and become slaves to their own creations. Maxwell never did.

Hamilton was very much his own man and expounded his own, sometimes contentious, views. He derided all attempts to 'prove' that God exists, holding that knowledge and logic, while essential tools for investigating the universe, were powerless to find its cause. James went along with this but had no doubt that Hamilton was wrong when he belittled mathematics. On safer ground, Hamilton agreed on most points with the Common Sense school but also respected the ideas of Immanuel Kant, Hume's German contemporary. He stressed Kant's proposition that all knowledge is relative: we know nothing about things except by their relationship to other things. This struck a powerful chord. It was not long before James was bringing such thoughts to bear on his scientific work. In an exercise for Hamilton on the properties of matter, James wrote:

> Now the only thing which can be directly perceived by the senses is Force, to which may be reduced light, heat, electricity, sound and all the other things which can be perceived by the senses.

Twenty years on, when James was checking a draft of Thomson and Tait's *Treatise on Natural Philosophy*, he had to correct them on this very point. They had defined mass incorrectly and had to be told 'matter is never perceived by the senses'. Lacking Maxwell's philosophical faculty, they had simply not turned their thoughts in the right direction. This little example gives us an idea of how Maxwell was able to explore regions of scientific thought that his contemporaries could not reach.

Maxwell's greatest work shows two unique characteristics which stem from his philosophical insight. The first is the way he could return to a subject, often after a gap of several years, and take it to new heights using an entirely fresh approach. He did this twice with electromagnetism. The second is even more remarkable. His electromagnetic theory embodied the notion that things we can measure directly, like mechanical force, are merely the outward manifestations of deeper processes, involving entities like electric field strength, which are beyond our powers of visualisation. This presages the view that twentieth century scientists came to. As Banesh Hoffmann puts it in *The Strange Story of the Quantum*: 'There is simply no way at all of picturing the fundamental atomic processes of nature in terms of space, time and causality'.

James was not just a thinker. He wanted to make experiments and was fortunate to have inspirational encouragement from James Forbes[1]. The two developed a rare rapport; James used to stay long after hours and was allowed to use the professor's laboratory to carry out all manner of investigations. Recognising the boy's talent and potential, Forbes simply let him follow his fancy. This was exactly the way James learnt best; he became expert in using the standard apparatus and in improvising his own when needed. The experience was so exhilarating that James later always tried to give his own research students similar freedom. Even when Director of the Cavendish Laboratory he never told people what research to do unless they asked him. 'I never try to dissuade a man from trying an experiment', he said to a friend, 'if he does not find what he wants he may find out something else'[2].

Forbes also helped to form the lucid literary style which characterised Maxwell's scientific writing. James had submitted a sloppily drafted paper to the Royal Society of Edinburgh and Forbes' mathematical colleague Philip Kelland was asked to referee it. Knowing that James needed to learn the lesson, Forbes undertook to deliver the critical comments himself. He pulled no punches: '... It is perfectly evident that it must be useless to

publish a paper for the use of scientific readers generally, the steps of which cannot, in many places, be followed by so expert an algebraist as Prof. Kelland ...'. The sharp reproof was an act of kindness and James knew it. He went on to develop a style of scientific writing that was all his own. Scholars find it as distinctive as others find the sound of Louis Armstrong's trumpet or the brushwork of Vincent van Gogh. The tone is authoritative but fresh and informal; the equations spring naturally from the arguments. Maxwell never managed to eliminate entirely his propensity to make algebraic slips and some found their way into his papers. Also, the concepts are in places so subtle and original that scholars still argue about exactly what Maxwell meant. Nevertheless, he left a superb body of published work, from which many of the standard texts used by today's physics and engineering students are derived.

Forbes was an all-round natural philosopher with a wide range of interests but his special passion was earth science, in which he was an energetic pioneer[3]. He invented the seismometer, measured the temperature of the earth at different depths, and was one of the first people to make a serious study of glaciers. For him, as for James, science was to be found everywhere. Sometimes, at weekends, he became a kind of scientific scoutmaster, taking the students on field trips, where boisterous joshing went along with serious endeavour. On one outing Forbes was uncharacteristically careless with his calibration: probably on purpose, to test the mettle of his young charges. James reports in a letter to Lewis Campbell:

> On Saturday, the natural philosophers ran up Arthur's Seat with the barometer. The Professor set it up at the top and let us pant at it till it ran down with drops. He did not set it straight, and made the hill grow fifty feet: but we got it down again.

Everything Forbes said or did on scientific topics was meat and drink to James, who was fascinated by the entire physical world. He already had keen observation and a flair for practical work;

under Forbes' influence these talents acquired discipline and professional poise. The inspiration that young James drew from Forbes is plainly seen in a book review he wrote many years later for the journal *Nature*:

> If a child has any latent talent for the study of nature, a visit to a real man of science at work in his laboratory may be a turning point in his life. He may not understand a word of what the man of science says to explain his operations; but he sees the operations themselves, and the pains and patience which are bestowed on them; and when they fail he sees how the man of science, instead of getting angry, searches for the cause of failure among the conditions of the operation.[4]

When his mentor died in 1868, James told a friend, 'I loved James Forbes'.

Not surprisingly, Forbes and Hamilton greatly outshone their fellow professors. Philip Kelland gave a useful mathematics course but James was not at all impressed by Professor Wilson's lectures in moral philosophy which, to his mind, served only to demonstrate that woolly thinking leads to wrong conclusions[5]. He enjoyed chemistry but thought it odd that lectures from Professor Gregory were given separately from practical chemistry sessions under Mr Kemp, particularly as 'Kemp the Practical' was apt to describe procedures taught by Gregory as 'useless and detrimental processes, invented by chemists who want something to do'. This experience helped to form Maxwell's conviction that practical work is not only essential to a proper scientific education but should be part and parcel of the lecture course, not tacked on as an afterthought.

The formal courses supplied only a small part of the knowledge James acquired during his 3 years at Edinburgh University. The rest came from reading and from making his own experiments. Much of this was done at Glenlair during the long vacation—in those days Scottish Universities closed from late April to early November so that students could go home to help with the farming. Among the many books he borrowed from the university library were Newton's *Opticks* and works by some of the great French mathematicians: Fourier's *Théorie analytique de la chaleur*, Monge's *Géometrie descriptive*, Cauchy's *Calcul differentiel* and Poisson's *Traité de mécanique*. He was so smitten by Fourier's book that he bought his own copy for 25 shillings, a considerable sum in 1849. In philosophy his reading included Thomas Hobbes' *Leviathan* and Adam Smith's *Theory of Moral Sentiments*. As well as all this there was some Latin and Greek, to keep his hand in, and novels and poetry for fun.

At Glenlair James spent a lot of time in an improvised laboratory-cum-workshop above the washhouse. Here he got together all the paraphernalia which the family called 'Jamesie's dirt'. He described the scene in a letter to Lewis Campbell:

> I have an old door set on two barrels, and two chairs, of which one is safe, and a skylight above, which will slide up and down.
>
> On the door (or table) there is a lot of bowls, jugs, plates, jam pigs*, etc., containing water, salt, soda, sulphuric acid, blue vitriol, plumbago ore; also broken glass, iron, and copper wire, copper and zinc plate, bees' wax, sealing wax, clay, rosin, charcoal, a lens, a Smee's Galvanic apparatus†, and a countless variety of little beetles, spiders and woodlice, which fall into the different liquids and poison themselves.

Sir Donald Bradman, greatest of all batsmen, used to say that he developed his superb eye and timing by spending hours as a boy hitting a golf ball against a wall with a cricket stump. James was doing something similar with his rough-and-ready experimenting.

He made crude electromagnetic devices. To make more batteries he electro-plated old jam jars with copper. He did chemical experiments and entertained the local children by

* Jars.

† An electrical kit, containing a battery.

letting them spit on a mixture of two white powders to turn it green.

But his chief fascination was with polarised light—light in which the wave vibrations are neatly lined up rather than being higgledy-piggledy[6]. He was enthralled by the beautiful coloured patterns that polarised light revealed in unannealed glass—glass which has been cooled quickly from red heat so that internal strains are 'frozen' into its structure, as the outer parts cool faster than the inner. The interest was not only aesthetic; he wanted to investigate the patterns of strain, or distortion, which gave rise to the colours. To get suitable glass he cut bits of ordinary window glass into geometrical shapes, heated them until they were red-hot and then cooled them rapidly.

At first he had no ready-made device for making polarised light and had to improvise. He knew that when ordinary light meets a glass surface at a certain angle, the part of the beam that is reflected is polarised. So he made a polariser using a large match box and two pieces of glass set with sealing wax at the correct angle. Another method was to pass light through a stack of 'polarising plates', thin slices of a crystalline material. To get suitable plates he spent hours patiently sawing and polishing strips of brittle saltpetre.

The coloured patterns turned out to be even more striking than expected. By ingenious jury-rigging he built a camera lucida, which made a virtual image of the coloured patterns appear on a piece of paper, so that he could copy them in watercolour. He sent some of the paintings to William Nicol, the famous optician whose workshop he had visited with his uncle John and Lewis Campbell 2 years before. Nicol was so impressed that he gave James a pair of his beautiful Iceland spar polarising prisms. James prized them all his life. For the task in hand they gave him a much easier and more reliable supply of polarised light.

There was more to do. Looking at pretty patterns in glass was all very well, but James saw it as a first step. Could the same method be used more generally to show up the patterns of strain in solid bodies of different shapes when put under different kinds

of mechanical stress—something of great interest to engineers? To test the idea James needed a transparent material that he could easily make into different shapes and then distort by stretching, squashing or twisting. How about jelly? It would not be amenable to stretching or squashing but it would be perfect for twisting, and all he needed was gelatine from the kitchen. He made a clear jelly in the shape of a thick ring, using a paper cylinder as the outer part of the mould and a cork as the inner. When it had set, he held the paper steady and applied torsional stress to the jelly by twisting the cork. Then he shone polarised light through the stressed cylinder of jelly and the strain patterns showed up beautifully. More jellies followed, twisted in different ways. This was the birth of the photoelastic method, which has been a boon to engineers—to try out the design of a component or structure they simply make a scale model from a transparent material, such as epoxy resin, and use polarised light to show the strain patterns under various loads.

These DIY adventures did much more than improve James' experimental skill; they helped to give him the deep feeling for nature's materials and processes that later pervaded all his theoretical work and was at least as important a part of that work as his mathematical ability.

There were also, of course, James' 'props'—mathematical investigations that took his fancy. Two of these were published while he was at Edinburgh University. Both were read to the Royal Society of Edinburgh by Philip Kelland because James was still considered too young to do so himself. The first followed naturally from his ovals paper of 3 years earlier. It was about the geometrical properties of the type of curve traced out by a point on one curve when it is rolled on another. An everyday example is the curve followed by a point on the outside of a bicycle wheel rolling on a flat road—an inverted U shape called a cycloid. One of the simpler results in James' paper is:

> If the curve A when rolled on a straight line produces a curve C, and if the curve A when rolled upon itself produces

the curve B, then the curve B when rolled upon the curve C will produce a straight line.

Intriguing stuff for geometers but not likely to have much practical application.

James' second paper was of a different order. It was an astonishing achievement for a 19 year-old working almost entirely on his own. The mathematics went hand-in-glove with his experiments using polarised light and dealt with the elasticity of solid bodies—the way they distort when put under stress. He set out for the first time the general mathematical theory of photo-elasticity based on strain functions, and derived the particular functions for cylinders, spheres and beams of various sections. James verified some of these results by his own experiments and illustrated the paper with carefully hand-coloured drawings of the strain patterns shown up by polarised light. He had worked hard on this paper but through inexperience sent in a draft which was tortuous to read because he had not taken enough trouble with the wording. At this point he received the strong rebuke from Forbes which has already been reported. James saw the fault at once and put the paper right. If his passage to scientific manhood can be marked down to a single episode, this was it.

Despite all this solitary activity, it was by no means a hermit's life for James at Glenlair. He delighted in the companionship of his father, who was in some ways more like an elder brother. He helped in the fields and passed time with the local lads. On hot days he tried to persuade them to join him swimming in the peat-brown pool where two rivers joined but they were afraid of the eels. He played with the estate children and organised them to fetch the water each morning. He joined in the 'Happy Valley' social life. But with so many thoughts and schemes whirring in his mind he longed for the chance to toss ideas around with friends. He wrote long letters to Lewis Campbell, describing his researches and his thoughts on philosophical issues and imploring him to visit.

For the first year at Edinburgh University he had enjoyed the company of his close friends from school. Then Lewis Campbell left for Oxford, and P. G. Tait and another friend, Allan Stewart, for Cambridge. He began to feel he was paddling in a backwater while they were striking out for exciting new shores. Perhaps he should, after all, prepare for a career at the Scottish Bar. He resolved to do some serious reading, but events then took a happy turn and he wrote jauntily to Campbell:

> I have notions of reading the whole of *Corpus Juris* and Pandects in no time at all; but these are getting somewhat dim, as the Cambridge scheme has been howked up from its repose in the region of abortions, and is as far forward as an inspection of the Cambridge *Calendar* and a communication with Cantabs.

John Clerk Maxwell had, at length, agreed that James should go to Cambridge. This was not the end of the matter, as there was also the choice of college. Forbes strongly recommended his alma mater, Trinity. P. G. Tait was already at St Peter's, known as Peterhouse, which was small and select, and Lewis Campbell's younger brother Robert was bound for Caius, which was highly regarded but so full that all freshmen had to lodge out. The decision went in favour of Peterhouse.

So James left for Cambridge at the age of 19. He had already acquired a vast store of knowledge on all manner of subjects, having read far more than most educated people read in a lifetime. He was an experienced experimenter and had published three mathematical papers. Yet he had not worked under any pressure; there was immense intellectual power in reserve.

His ways were still odd. He had kept his Galloway accent. In strange company he was deeply reserved but when at ease with friends he would be the hub of the group, delighting them with genial banter and a flow of thought-provoking ideas on any topic. He dressed tidily but with no notion of smartness, still less fashion. He was indifferent to any kind of luxury, preferring to travel third class on the railway because he liked a hard seat. Lewis Campbell's mother summed him up in her diary:

> His manners are very peculiar; but having good sense, sterling worth, and good humour, the intercourse with a college will rub off his oddities. I doubt not of his being a distinguished man.

It was arranged that James would take rooms in Peterhouse, Cambridge, on 18 October 1850.

CHAPTER FOUR

LEARNING TO JUGGLE

Cambridge 1850–1854

James travelled down with his father. They decided to stop on the way to visit Peterborough and Ely cathedrals, where they got chatting with other tourists. The talk of the day was a project then afoot to drain the Wash and settle the new land, to be called Victoria county—a plan that evidently went the way of many other 'best laid schemes o' mice an' men'.

On arriving in Cambridge James was as excited as any new student. He reported to his tutor at Peterhouse and, to his joy, managed to get rooms with good light, where he unpacked a collection of bits and pieces from his Glenlair den, including magnets, unannealed glass, gelatine, gutta percha* and his Nicol prisms. To crown his contentment, he was able to invite his old friend Tait in for tea and they caught up lost time with a long chat. The next morning he was taken with other newcomers on a tour of the colleges, which included homage at the statues of Isaac Newton and Francis Bacon in Trinity College Chapel. He was amused to see an example of petty officialdom—a notice in the College hall threatening expulsion to anyone who visited some stables which had been set up on College land in defiance of a ban made because of the 'immoral nature of the establishment'.

* An Asian vegetable gum, similar to rubber. It was used in golf balls and for electrical insulation, and has interesting optical properties.

Cambridge was beautiful, and replete with the tradition of scholarship. He was in high spirits. But there were soon some echoes of early days at school. At lectures he found himself covering dull old ground, 'spelling out Euclid' and 'monotonously parsing a Greek play'. Fellow freshmen at Peterhouse were serious about their studies, as he was, but not inclined to listen to his ideas or join in the kind of expansive discussion he enjoyed. He began to think of 'migrating' to another college, perhaps Trinity, of which Forbes had spoken so highly. At the same time his father—an assiduous networker—was hearing things that made him worry that James might find it hard to get a fellowship at Peterhouse after his degree course. The college had turned out more than its share of high achievers and was a magnet for students with mathematical talent but it was small and had a relatively modest financial endowment. There would probably be only one suitable fellowship open to men in James' year, and the competition included E. J. Routh, who already had a reputation as a prodigious mathematician. The outcome was that James moved to Trinity after one term.

Life at Trinity was far more congenial. It was a large and sociable college and he quickly made friends, mostly among the classics students. Boisterous talk ran the gamut of young men's interests, from deep issues in theology and moral philosophy to whist, chess, the Newmarket horse races and, no doubt, girls—although, sadly, sources shed little light on this aspect. The master of Trinity at this time was William Whewell (pronounced 'hyoowel'), the carpenter's son from Lancashire who had become a celebrated polymath, and under his inspirational tutelage the college had become the most fertile ground imaginable for debating ideas on all manner of topics. James was in his element. He joined in discussions on just about anything and often drew on his vast and reflective reading to give a surprising new angle to the conversation. Some evenings he went 'prowling', looking for fellow students to exchange ideas with and met others doing the same.

Among the myriad topics of debate there was one which probed deep into James' inner feelings—science versus religion.

From both sides people argued that the two were incompatible. Those like James who believed them complementary felt a need to explain their position, at least to themselves. It was at Trinity that James came to adopt a way of resolving the inner conflict that was to serve him well for the rest of his life. His faith was too deeply rooted to be shaken but his probing mind would not allow any possible fissures between God and science to remain unexplored; they had to be surveyed and bridged. This was an intensely personal process, to be re-examined in the light of each new scientific discovery, whether his own or someone else's. He summarised it many years later when replying to an invitation to join the Victoria Institute, an eminent organisation specifically set up to establish common ground between Christianity and science. Over the years he had turned them down several times, but they were so keen to have him in their number that in 1875 the President and Council sent him a special request to join. He declined once more, explaining:

> ... I think that the results which each man arrives at in his attempts to harmonise his science with his Christianity ought not to be regarded as having any significance except to the man himself, and to him only for a time, and should not receive the stamp of a society. For it is in the nature of science, especially those branches of science which are spreading into unknown regions, to be continually changing*.

For all his erudition, and his ability to devise formulae to explain the physical world, Maxwell clearly believed he was no better qualified than anyone else to explain the relationship between the physical and spiritual worlds.

A more light-hearted topic was the so-called occult sciences, which at that time included the craze of 'table turning'—when several people placed their hands on a table it would move as

* The surviving draft ends at 'continually' but the final 'changing' is clearly implied.

though propelled by mystic powers. James and his friends dabbled in such things for fun, but beneath the hilarity lay something disturbing. He began to be worried that so many people were ready to accept claims that dark forces were at work, and that no-one could explain what caused this gullibility. He put his view, rather enigmatically, in a letter to a friend.

> ... I see daily more reason to believe that the study of the 'dark sciences' is one which will repay investigation. I think that what is called the proneness to superstition in the present day is much more significant than some make it. The prevalence of a misdirected tendency proves the misdirection of a prevalent tendency. It is the nature and object of this tendency that calls for examination.[1]

Many people today worry about the same thing and Maxwell would surely be pleased that the brief has been taken up by the eminent American scientist and writer Carl Sagan in his book *The Demon-haunted World.*

James' private reading continued apace and he gave full rein to his poetic muse, yet he always finished whatever work was set by lecturers. With so much to fit in he tried unusual daily routines. One involved jogging in the middle of the night. A fellow student reports:

> From 2 to 2.30 a.m. he took exercise by running along the upper corridor, down the stairs, along the lower corridor, then up the stairs, and so on until the inhabitants of the rooms along his track got up and lay *perdus* behind their sporting-doors to have shots at him with boots, hair-brushes, etc., as he passed.

Not all of Maxwell's experiments worked!

He found himself having to turn down many of the supper party invitations that came along, simply to stop things getting out of hand. But he did not refuse an invitation to join the Apostles—formally the Select Essay Club—a group of 12 students who considered themselves the crème de la crème and chose their own new members each year to replace those who had left. They took turns to host meetings where, after tea, one member would read a essay on any subject; discussion would follow and the members would then record their opinions in the club records. The Apostles were indeed an élite group: over the years, their members have included Alfred Tennyson, Bertrand Russell, Lytton Strachey and John Maynard Keynes. Young men who could already think, write and talk very well had the chance to spar with their peers. The essays generally had more style than substance; they were a chance to show off and practise one's craft at the same time. But they also encouraged the essayist to stretch his own thinking in an uninhibited way and provoke constructive reactions.

James took this opportunity to the full and did not spare his fellow members any of the scientific or philosophical issues which gripped him. In his essay *Analogies* he points out that we need both data and theory to make sense of the world:

> ... The dimmed outlines of phenomenal things all merge into one another unless we put on the focusing glass of theory, and screw it up sometimes to one pitch of definition and sometimes to another, so as to see down into different depths through the great millstone of the world.

As good a 49 word summary as you can get of Maxwell's scientific philosophy.

Another essay was *Is Autobiography possible?* Here he makes clear his view that introspection should not be performed in public:

> ... When a man once begins to make a theory of himself, he generally succeeds in making himself into a theory.

> ... The stomach pump of the confessional ought to be used only in cases of manifest poisoning. More gentle remedies are better for the constitution in ordinary cases.

Goodness knows what Maxwell would make of our current relish for watching people indulging in histrionic self-exposure on television. He would certainly have a wry smile at the irony of the fact that his own electromagnetic theory provides the means of bringing such unwholesome displays into our homes.

James wrote dozens of poems while at Trinity, from translations of Greek and Latin epic odes to scraps of verse dashed off on a whim to amuse his friends. Two which were certainly intended as ephemeral have become possibly the best remembered of all. In the first, the unfortunate butt of James' pen was the officious Senior Dean, who was leaving to become Rector of Shillington—for years he had sent fussy notes to anyone who missed a chapel service or went incorrectly dressed. It is a parody of Robert Burns' *John Anderson*:

John Alexander Frere, John,
  When we were first acquent,
You lectured us as Freshmen
  In the holy term of Lent;
But now you're gettin' bald, John,
  Your end is drawing near,
And I think we'd better say 'Goodbye,
  John Alexander Frere'.

. . .

The Lecture Room no more, John,
  Shall hear thy drowsy tone,
No more shall men in Chapel
  Bow down before thy throne.
But Shillington with meekness
  The Oracle shall hear,
That sent St Mary's all to sleep—
  John Alexander Frere.

Then once before we part, John,
  Let all be clean forgot,
Our scandalous inventions,
  Thy note-lets, prized or not.
For under all conventions,

The small man lived sincere,
The kernel of the Senior Dean,
John Alexander Frere.[2]

This is as close as Maxwell ever got to mockery in his verses. He was usually much closer to W. S. Gilbert than to Tom Lehrer. The 'sincere' was a genuine tribute: sincerity was a quality Maxwell prized above all others.

In the second, James takes the part of the 'rigid body' beloved of lecturers and problem setters in what we would now call applied mathematics, and offers an irreverent view of the proceedings from its own perspective. Burns again, this time *Comin' through the Rye*.

Gin a body meet a body
Flyin' through the air
Gin a body hit a body,
Will it fly? And where?
Ilka impact has its measure.
Ne'er a ane hae I,
Yet a' the lads they measure me,
Or, at least, they try.

Gin a body meet a body
Altogether free,
How they travel afterwards
We do not always see,
Ilka problem has its method
By analytics high;
For me, I ken na ane o' them,
But what the waur am I?

When time allowed, James tinkered with his motley collection of scientific apparatus, building up ideas for more serious investigation later. Other ideas came from everyday incidents, and from two of these he wrote short articles. The first was prompted when he noticed that when bits of paper are thrown into the air they fall with a particular form of dancing flight—a brief haphazard fluttering followed by steady spinning at a fixed angle to the vertical. The second article reported his remarkable discovery of the fish-eye lens, by legend inspired by close examination of a kipper at breakfast. His idea was that a flat lens with a variable refractive index would, unlike normal lenses, form a perfect image; James gave the formula by which the index would have to vary to make this happen.

Not being allowed to keep a dog in College, he made friends with the house cats and persuaded them to let him drop them onto his bed to find out from how low a height they would still land on their feet. Raconteurs took this story and embellished it. Visiting Cambridge some years later, James had to deny that he used to throw cats out of windows.

Cambridge's reputation as a training ground for future high-court judges and archbishops was founded principally upon the Mathematical Tripos exam. Even students of Greek and Latin had to pass the Tripos to get a degree. It was a fearsome exam, held in a chilly hall in January in the last year of the 4 year course. Everyone sat the first 3 days' papers, which were on standard bookwork. Those who wanted an honours degree, including classics students, had to endure a further 4 days of more difficult problems. The reward for the wranglers—those who got first class honours—was lifelong recognition and a sustained boost in whatever career they chose. They were ranked by number, and to become senior (first) wrangler was like winning an Olympic gold medal. Straight after the Tripos, the best mathematicians took a still more difficult exam for the Smith's Prize, which carried immense professional kudos.

The mathematical tradition derived chiefly from the great Isaac Newton, who had been both student and professor at Cambridge and had created the science of mechanics with his laws of motion and his introduction of the differential calculus to deal with quantities that vary continuously. Newton's methods were based on geometry rather than algebra and so the Tripos syllabus included the work of Euclid, the Ancient Greek founder of geometry. So revered was Newton that for many years the Tripos question-setters completely ignored the huge advances being made by French mathematicians such as Legendre, Lagrange, Laplace, Cauchy, Monge, Fourier and Poisson, and others like Euler from Switzerland and, the greatest of all, Gauss from Germany. Eventually they realised they were being left behind and, by James' time, had recovered most of the ground, thanks to the efforts of a small group including Charles Babbage, now chiefly remembered as father of the computer[3].

The Tripos questions demanded virtuosity in the art of solving problems quickly. In fact they were designed specifically for this purpose, like crossword puzzles, and rarely bore relation to real-life problems—a fault that Maxwell strove to correct when he later became an examiner. To answer questions accurately and fast, one had to master a welter of tricks and short-cuts, and avoid mistakes. This was not James' strong suit; he was a bit like a trapeze artist having to learn juggling tricks. But he knew what he was letting himself in for and set out to learn, in his words, 'that knack of solving problems which Prof. Forbes has taught me to despise'.

He joined the tutor group of the renowned 'wrangler maker' William Hopkins[4]. Most of the Tripos coaches, including Hopkins, worked freelance; so their income depended on sustaining a reputation for driving students to good results. Hopkins was mightily impressed by James' knowledge but appalled by what he saw as its 'state of disorder'. He set out to bring more method to James' freewheeling way of tackling maths questions. James did indeed learn how to juggle but was reluctant to restrict his repertoire to the standard tricks. Wherever possible, he tried to picture the problem. On at least one occasion when the tutor had filled the blackboard with symbols and numbers James solved the problem in a few lines with a diagram. He reduced, but failed to eradicate, his tendency to make algebraic errors. Hopkins reported: 'It is not possible for that man to think incorrectly on physical subjects; in his analysis, however, he is far more deficient'. James did not shirk the work but spent no more time on it than needed; he never went in for the intense cramming that was reckoned to be essential for high honours in the Tripos. As his friend P. G. Tait later put it, 'the pupil to a great extent took his own way'.

One of the other members of the group, W. N. Lawson, gives a picture of James at this time.

> Maxwell was, I daresay you remember, very fond of a talk upon almost anything. He and I were pupils (at an enormous distance apart) of Hopkins, and I well recollect how, when I had been working all the night before and all the morning at Hopkins' problems with little or no result, Maxwell would come in for a gossip, and talk on and on while I was wishing him far away, till at last, about half an hour before our meeting at Hopkins's, he would say—'Well, I must go to old Hop's problems'; and by the time we met they were all done.

James was generous with his time to any friend who needed it—as well as to some, like Lawson, who did not! When one friend had eye trouble and could not read, James spent an hour each evening reading out his bookwork for the next day. He bucked up fellow students when they were depressed and on several occasions nursed others who were sick. He helped freshmen who were having trouble with their studies. He also found time to keep up a lively correspondence with his father, Aunt Jane, Lewis Campbell and others.

Perhaps he overdid things; while on a vacation visit to the family of a friend in Suffolk he was taken ill with a fever, became delirious and was laid up for 2 weeks[5]. The family looked after him as one of their own. He was profoundly grateful and greatly moved by their kindness, particularly as they had taken the trouble to write to his father with daily reports. For all this, he could not help making a philosophical observation on their mode of family life: everyone was so solicitous of everyone else's wishes that no-one had any life of their own. He put his own, rather different, guide to domestic Utopia in a letter to a friend.

> Let each member of the family be allowed some little province of thought, work, or study, which is not to be too much

inquired into or sympathised with or encouraged by the rest, and let the limits of this be enlarged till he has a wide, free field of independent action, which increases the resources of the family so much more as it is peculiarly his own.

A few months before James' Tripos exam, he was on the fringe of a widely debated religious controversy. One of the fellows of King's College, F. D. Maurice, had attracted a following among the undergraduates with his Christian Socialist movement. Hating what he saw as the dehumanising effect of industrial work under capitalism, Maurice advocated cooperatives and the setting up of Working Men's Colleges. He published his views in a set of *Theological Essays*. All this alarmed the University establishment. Looking for a pretext to dismiss him, they examined the *Theological Essays* for possible violations of the Articles of the Church of England, which all fellows were required to uphold. They found their grounds and Maurice was sacked.

Along with several friends and many other students throughout the University, James was appalled at Maurice's treatment. He did not go along with Maurice's rather doctrinaire approach to theology but supported to the hilt the idea of colleges for working men. Students did not march or sit-in in those days and the dismissal passed without public incident, but feelings ran deep and the influence of Maurice's missionary zeal remained in Cambridge long after his going. James had already helped young farm workers at home by lending them books from the Glenlair library. Later, as a fellow at Cambridge and then as a professor at Aberdeen and at King's College, London, he gave up at least one evening a week to teach at Working Men's Colleges.

The exams came. Students had been drilled in hard and sustained writing so they could keep it up for 6 hours a day throughout the 7 day Tripos exam. It was both a physical and a mental ordeal. Some form of restorative relaxation was essential in the evenings, and here James found himself providing an unusual service. The usual occupations of talking and reading did not quite fill the bill, but some students found the ideal alternative by crowding into James' rooms and dabbling in experiments with magnets under his amiable instruction.

In the Tripos James came second to E. J. Routh of Peterhouse. In the competition for the Smith's Prize they were declared joint winners. Routh was a specialist mathematician and a very good one; he went on to do first-rate research and now has his name commemorated in a mathematical function, the routhian, which sits happily alongside its illustrious companions the lagrangian and the hamiltonian. James had done well—not quite as well as P. G. Tait, who had been senior wrangler and Smith's Prize winner 2 years earlier—but Tait had not been up against Routh. He had established his credentials and could now expect to gain a fellowship at Trinity, which would be an excellent start to the kind of working life he wanted. His father was delighted, and congratulations came in from uncles and aunts and his friends in Edinburgh.

It had been a happy 4 years. He had given full rein to his free-ranging intellectual spirit but still completed the Tripos grind with honour. He had absorbed the Cambridge student tradition and left his own stamp on it in return. And he had grown up—his ways were still out of the ordinary but he now impressed new acquaintances as an interesting young man, rather than merely an odd one. Most of all, he had formed a number of deep and lasting friendships. Among these friends were R. H. Pomeroy, a genial giant of a man from Ireland who joined the Indian Civil Service, R. B. Litchfield, who ran the Working Men's College in London, and H. M. Butler, who became Headmaster of Harrow and, later, Master of Trinity. James made a profound impression on many besides his close friends, not so much because he had the mark of genius as because he was simply a good man who made them feel better about themselves and about the world in general. Another student, who was not a particular friend, later gave Lewis Campbell his memory of James at college:

> Of Maxwell's geniality and kindness of heart you will have had many instances. Everyone who knew him at Trinity

> can recall some kindness or some act of his which left an ineffaceable impression of his goodness on the memory—for 'good' Maxwell was in the best sense of that word.

Campbell himself gives a picture of James as his friends saw him:

> His presence had by this time fully acquired the unspeakable charm for all who knew him which made him insensibly become the centre of any circle, large or small, consisting of his friends or kindred.

The immediate future was settled. He would stay at Trinity as a bachelor-scholar and apply for a fellowship, which he should gain within a couple of years. After a few years as a fellow he would look for a professorship, probably at another university—in those days fellows of Trinity were required to be ordained into the Church of England within 7 years of appointment and to remain unmarried, and James had no intention of making either commitment. He wanted to explore new ground in science and was confident in his ability. The prospect was exhilarating.

CHAPTER FIVE

BLUE AND YELLOW MAKE PINK

Cambridge 1854–1856

Tripos duty done, James was free to develop all the ideas that had been spinning away at the back of his mind for the last 4 years. And he was now in full command of the tools of his trade: through Hopkins his mathematics had acquired the same discipline and poise that Forbes had earlier brought to his experimental work. There were duties—his new status as bachelor-scholar qualified him to take pupils—and he would soon need to take another exam for the fellowship, but there was plenty of time for his own research and he enjoyed variety. Indeed, he took on extra teaching and examining work; it would be good practice for a professorship later on. He also took plenty of exercise: walking, rowing on the river Cam, strenuous sessions in the new gymnasium, and swimming in the 'bathing shed', where he helped to organise a club to make things more sociable. Like many young people on the threshold of an independent career, he had thoughts on how to make the most of life. James wrote his down:

> He that would enjoy life and act with freedom must have the work of the day continually before his eyes. Not yesterday's work, lest he fall into despair, nor tomorrow's, less he become a visionary—not that which ends with the day, which is a worldly work, nor yet that only which remains to eternity, for by it he cannot shape his actions.

Happy is the man who can recognise in the work of Today a connected portion of the work of life, and an embodiment of the work of Eternity ...

James was not given to solemn aphorisms. These words were by no means intended for public instruction; they were simply thoughts he had jotted down to clear his mind. That done, he passed them on to a friend who was about to take up work as a schoolmaster and had asked for advice. We assume the friend found them useful because he kept them for many years. He was F. W. Farrar, who became Headmaster of Marlborough School and later Dean of Canterbury but is mainly remembered as a prolific author, whose books include the popular moral tale *Eric, or Little by Little*.

There were two aspects of the physical world that James particularly wanted to explore. Neither was well understood. One was electricity and magnetism, and we shall come to that. The other was the process of vision, in particular the way we see colours—harking back to his question as a 3 year-old, 'but how d'ye *know* it's blue?'.

One way to investigate vision would be to look into human and animal eyes. As there were no instruments to do this, he made one. This was close to being the world's first ophthalmoscope—credit for the invention usually goes to the German physicist and physiologist Hermann Helmholtz[1], who produced his prototype independently a year or so earlier. People were chary at first about having a strange instrument pointed at their eyes, but James had a way with dogs and soon had several canine helpers. He found dogs' eyes to be 'very beautiful behind, a copper-coloured ground, with glorious bright patches and networks of blue, yellow and green, with blood vessels great and small'. People were still reluctant but he managed to persuade some to let him look in by showing them his own eye first. Human eyes were less spectacular than dogs', plain dark brown, but showed the image of a candle flame clearly. It would be interesting to test people's vision in different parts of the retina, particularly in a mysterious yellow spot near the centre, but first there was a more fundamental problem to be solved. No-one had yet managed to explain how colour vision worked.

Isaac Newton had shown in the seventeenth century that sunlight, which we see as white, was an even mixture of all the colours in the solar spectrum, which range from red to violet, as displayed in a rainbow. Some colours, for example brown, do not appear in the spectrum but Newton reasoned that they must all be mixtures of pure spectral colours. The problem was to find the rules governing the mixing process—how much of which spectral colours had to be mixed together to give a particular non-spectral colour? Newton came up with an ingenious imaginary model. He started by setting all the colours of the spectrum in a circle and then placed weights at appropriate places on the circle to represent the colours present in a particular mixture, the value of each weight being in proportion to the amount of its colour in the mix. Every non-spectral colour lay inside the circle and its position was simply the centre of gravity of the weights representing the mix of spectral colours that made it up. White lay at the centre of the circle because it was an even mix of all the colours in the spectrum. This construction was a brilliant improvisation but Newton knew it could not be quite right. For one thing, there was the awkward point of discontinuity on the circle where the colours at the opposite ends of the spectrum, red and violet, butted together.

For a century and a half, Newton's explanation was the best available but, in a sense, art was ahead of science in this field. Painters had long known how to mix colours on their palettes: they often used red, blue and yellow as 'primary' colours and mixed them in different proportions to get the colour they wanted. And textile makers mixed dyes in a similar way to make new colours. Perhaps there was some physiological significance in the *number* of primary colours—three? Someone who thought so was the English doctor and physicist Thomas Young. In the early nineteenth century he had proposed that the human eye has three types of receptor, each of which is sensitive to a particular colour, and that messages from them are combined by the brain to give a single *perceived* colour. This was a brilliant insight but Young was not able to follow it through with proof and the theory lay largely neglected until the time of our story.

James' interest in colour vision had started in James Forbes' laboratory when he was a student at Edinburgh University. Forbes had the idea of mixing colours by taking a disc marked with coloured sectors like a pie-chart and spinning it fast. The eye and brain then cannot react quickly enough to see the individual colours; instead one sees a blurred-out mix which the brain interprets as a single, different, colour. Forbes reasoned that, if Young's theory was right, it ought to be possible to produce any desired colour, including white, by choosing three appropriate primary colours, arranging them in sectors on the disc and then varying the sizes of the sectors until the appropriate mix had been found. He tried to get white by mixing red, yellow and blue—the artists' ingredients. But no mixture of red, yellow and blue gave white. Perplexed, he tried mixing just two colours, blue and yellow, to check that they gave green: a well-known rule for mixing paints and dyes. He was surprised when he spun the disc to see not green but a dull *pink*.

This was perplexing but James began to experiment on his own and soon found the explanation. There is a fundamental difference between mixing lights, as when spinning a multi-coloured disc, and mixing pigments, as one does with paints and dyes. The pigments act as extractors of colour, so that the light you see after mixing two paints is whatever colour the paints have failed to absorb. In other words, mixing pigments is a subtractive process, whereas mixing lights is additive. All this is now standard fare for physics students but it was ground-breaking work in the 1850s. When James tried spinning a disc using red, *green* and blue as primaries it all worked beautifully.

Now was the time to try to set the results on a proper footing. Forbes had been forced by ill-health to give up experimental work, so James was on his own. He used a modified form of spinning disc in the form of a top, and ordered sheets of coloured paper from D. R. Hay, the Edinburgh artist and printer who had been so interested in James' paper on oval curves. Hay was probably the country's leading expert on colour printing and could supply a wide range of colours. James cut discs from the coloured sheets and made a hole in the middle of each to accommodate the spindle of the top. To get the pie-chart effect, he slit the discs radially so that three, or more if needed, could be overlapped and slotted together on the spindle with any desired amount of each colour showing. Using a circular scale around the rim of the top, he could measure the percentage of each colour in the mix. When the top was spun, the combined colour was matched against a differently coloured paper held alongside. This device began to yield interesting results but then James thought of an improvement. He mounted a second, smaller, set of paper discs on top of the first so that when the top was spun he could get a match by adjusting the discs until the colour of the inner circle was identical to that of the outer ring. This not only gave better matching but enabled him to match the brightness of the colours, as well as their hues, by including a black sector in either the inner or outer part[2].

It was good fun spinning away and mixing colours but James wanted to find a system for defining how any one colour was related to all the others. He found one, the Maxwell colour triangle (Figure 1). This was a great discovery[3].

The three primary colours, red, green and blue are represented, as in Figure 1, by the vertices R, G and B of an equilateral triangle[4]. Each point inside the triangle corresponds to a colour which can be obtained by mixing red, green and blue; the proportions of the mix are given by the relative lengths of the coordinates r, g and b. For example the point C in Figure 1 represents a colour formed from about nine parts of red to four of green to three of blue—by the author's rough calculation a dusky pink. White is represented by the point W in the middle. Brightness, or intensity, is not shown in the triangle, but can be specified by an extra number and represented geometrically, if

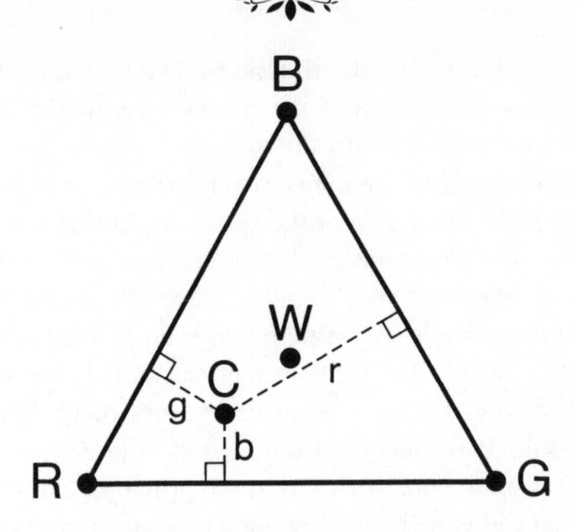

Figure 1 Maxwell's colour triangle

R, G, and B represent the primary colours red, green and blue
W represents white (an equal mixture of red, green and blue)
r, g and b represent the red, green and blue components of any other colour, C

needed, by extending the diagram to three dimensions. Along with the triangle went a simple equation:

$$\text{colour matched} = x\% \text{ of red} + y\% \text{ of green} + z\% \text{ of blue}$$

where $x = 100\mathrm{r}/(\mathrm{r}+\mathrm{g}+\mathrm{b})$, $y = 100\mathrm{g}/(\mathrm{r}+\mathrm{g}+\mathrm{b})$ and $z = 100\mathrm{b}/(\mathrm{r}+\mathrm{g}+\mathrm{b})$.

James was faced with a problem: not all colours could be matched by a simple mix of his red, green and blue primaries. There were two reasons: first, he did not know exactly which three colours the eye's three types of receptor were most sensitive to (and had no means of finding out); and second, although each receptor was most sensitive to a particular colour it would also receive a band of neighbouring colours, just as a radio set receives a band of frequencies on either side of the one it is tuned to. Whatever choices of particular shades of red, green and blue he made, they would not match the eye's receptors exactly and consequently not all colours would fall within the triangle. But he met the challenge with a simple and ingenious solution. He found when spinning his disc that he could match the remaining colours by combining one of the primaries with the colour to be matched rather than with the other two primaries—in other words he put a *negative* component of one primary into the mix by putting it on the other side of the equation. In this way he was able to plot all colours on his diagram: those with a negative value of one primary had a negative value of r or g or b and so lay *outside* the triangle. His system was robust: it did not depend on choosing exactly the right primary colours. The closer the primaries accorded with the eye's characteristics, the fewer colours would lie outside the triangle but, as James pointed out, the system would work with any three primary colours as long as one could get white by mixing them in some proportion.

He went on to show that the representation of a perceived colour as a mixture of three primaries was equivalent to an alternative scheme proposed by Hermann Grassmann, in which the colour is principally defined by two variables, now called spectral hue and saturation. In Figure 1, hue is determined by the direction of a line drawn from W to C, and saturation by its length. He showed that to convert values from one system to the other is a matter of simple geometry, so it is now easy for colour technicians to switch from one to the other as needed. To complete the specification of a colour, both systems bring in intensity, or brightness, as a third variable.

Maxwell's triangle is used today in a form called a chromaticity diagram, which differs only in detail from his original concept. The diagram uses a right-angled triangle in which the proportions of red and green are plotted, the blue component being implied because the proportions of red, green and blue always add up to 1. As in Figure 1, brightness, or intensity, is not shown, but it can be specified by a number which could be represented in the diagram by recourse to a third dimension.

James got his friends and colleagues to have a go at matching colours and found that there is remarkably little variation in colour perception among people with normal vision. He particularly sought out colour-blind people and found that most of them lacked the red-sensitive receptors, which explained why they could not tell red from green. He came up with a remedy: spectacles with one red lens and one green—they did not catch on!

The work was a tour-de-force. James had swept a sea of confusion and doubt aside. He had verified the three-component theory of colour vision and given the world a simple and reliable mathematical recipe for combining colours. But the announcement was modest, even for those days; James simply posted off a paper to the Royal Society of Edinburgh[5] and gave a talk to the Cambridge Philosophical Society, where he demonstrated some of the results, using the colour top.

Nowadays we get daily proof of the three-component theory—colour television works on exactly this principle. But Maxwell's name is rarely mentioned in this connection. One reason is that Helmholtz was working independently on the same topic at the same time and, through the wayward channels of posterity, has been given more of the credit. At least one authoritative writer has given the opinion that Maxwell should get higher billing, but priority disputes are tedious and form no part of our story[6].

In any case, no thoughts of glory entered James' head. He was concerned that the job was far from finished. He wanted to measure the variation in people's eyesight more accurately and get precise values for the combinations of red, green and blue which matched the range of pure spectral colours. The colour top was too imprecise for this kind of work. Although it allowed accurate matching, the colours on the discs were not expressly defined. They were, as he put it, 'simply specimens of different kinds of paint'. To get results that other people could replicate, he would have to extract pure colours directly from sunlight, and combine them. Never at a loss for invention, he devised a 'colour box' which did this, using prisms to spread the sunlight into its component colours and adjustable slits to select the colours he wanted and regulate the amount of each colour. James had already realised that some such device would be needed at some stage and had made a primitive 'colour box' in his Glenlair den while on vacation from Edinburgh University.

He now set about making an improved version, work which would bear fruit later.

At the same time, he was getting to grips with electricity and magnetism, and in 1855 produced what many historians regard as his first 'great' paper. It was the first of three papers, spread over 9 years, which brought about a revolution not only in electricity and magnetism but in the way scientists think about the whole physical world.

Thanks to the work of Coulomb, Ampère, Faraday and others, quite a lot was known about the phenomena of electricity and magnetism. Volumes had been written, but the knowledge was fragmented; there was no theory that adequately explained how everything fitted together. Before he could come to any kind of plan of action James had to do a great deal of reading, much of it highly mathematical. This was, in his words, 'a process of simplification and reduction of previous results to a form in which the mind can grasp them'. If even Maxwell had to struggle to make sense of the situation, it is small wonder that no-one had yet come up with a unifying theory.

What were the 'previous results'? There were many but all were related to four main effects which had been clearly demonstrated by experiment. First, electric charges attract or repel one another with a force inversely proportional to the square of the distance between them: unlike charges attract, like ones repel. Second, magnetic poles attract or repel one another in a similar way but always come in pairs: every north pole is yoked to a south pole[7]. Third, an electric current in a wire creates a circular magnetic field around the wire, its direction depending on that of the current. Fourth, a current is induced in a loop of wire when it is moved towards or away from a magnet, or a magnet is moved towards or away from it, the direction of the current depending on that of the movement.

There were two ways in which scientists tried to explain these and related effects. Mathematically inclined physicists, like the Frenchmen Siméon-Denis Poisson and André-Marie Ampère, and the German Wilhelm Weber, had derived equations on the assumption that electrical charges and magnetic poles act on one another *at a distance* and that nothing happens in the space between them. Michael Faraday, on the other hand, believed that electrical charges and magnets infuse all space with *lines of force*, which interact with the lines of force emanating from other charges and magnets to produce the electrical and magnetic forces that we experience.

Most prominent scientists of the day strongly favoured the action at a distance idea: although it had not yet provided an authoritative explanation for all the known effects, it had enabled precise formulae to be derived and these worked well. And it followed the well-established model of Newton's theory of gravitation. Their judgement was strengthened by a widely-held belief that the great Newton had explicitly rejected the possibility of gravity acting through some kind of medium, rather than by direct action at a distance. Newton was a reluctant and irascible communicator and clearly had given some of his contemporaries grounds to interpret his thoughts in that way. But he actually took the opposite view, as is clear from this passage from a letter he wrote to a colleague:

> That gravity should be innate, inherent, and essential to matter, so that one body can act on another at a distance, through a vacuum, without the mediation of anything else, by and through which their action and force may be conveyed from one to another, is to me so great an absurdity, that I believe no man, who has in philosophical matters a competent faculty of thinking, can ever fall into it.[8]

A pretty irony. The folk-hero of the action-at-a-distance school would have taken Faraday's side! But their views were entrenched. Some went as far as to ridicule Faraday: Sir George Airy, the Astronomer Royal, gave his opinion:

> I can hardly imagine anyone who practically and numerically knows the agreement [between calculations based on action

> at a distance and experimental results] to hesitate an instant between this simple and precise action on the one hand and anything so vague and varying as lines of force on the other.

Michael Faraday is, along with James Clerk Maxwell, among the greatest scientists who have ever lived. Born 43 years before Maxwell into a poor family and apprenticed at 14 to a bookbinder, he gleaned whatever knowledge he could from books brought in for binding and was fascinated by the science articles in an encyclopaedia. Eventually he had the confidence to join the local philosophical society, where he took notes of all the talks and bound them into quarto volumes. He then took the slenderest opportunity when a kind customer, impressed by the young man's enterprise, gave him a ticket to some lectures by the brilliant and charismatic Sir Humphry Davy at the Royal Institution in London. Enthralled by the talks, Faraday wrote them up and sent a bound copy to Davy, asking for a job. After a year or so he got one, when Davy had to sack one of his staff for fighting. He started as a bottle-washer and learned the trade of experimenting—a second apprenticeship, but this time at his true vocation. Davy made him his assistant but became jealous when his protégé began to look more like a rival. There were arguments but the acrimony was all on Davy's side; Faraday revered him to the end.

After Davy died Faraday was appointed Professor at the Royal Institution, a post he held until his death 34 years later. In that time he performed and published a vast number of experiments, mostly in chemistry and in electricity and magnetism. From keen observation, meticulous attention to detail and sheer persistence he developed a commanding insight into physical processes and produced a scintillating run of discoveries. He was also, in his quiet way, a showman and carried on Davy's tradition by drawing full-capacity audiences to his lectures. By 1840 he was probably the most celebrated scientist in Britain. But he was never part of the scientific establishment. He had never been to a decent school, let alone a university, and was completely lacking in mathematics. Everyone marvelled at his experimental genius, but few placed equal value on his ability as a theoretician.

Maxwell was one who did. Reading through Faraday's *Experimental Researches*, James was struck at first by Faraday's openness and integrity:

> Faraday ... shows us his unsuccessful as well as his successful experiments, and his crude ideas as well as his developed ones, and the reader, however inferior to him in inductive power, feels sympathy even more than admiration, and is tempted to believe that, if he had the opportunity, he too would be a discoverer.[9]

Reading further, James came more and more to recognise the power of Faraday's thinking. The great man's modest description of his task as 'working, finishing, publishing' gave no idea of the intellectual strength and subtlety which pervaded his work. Discoveries had not come easily: great leaps of imaginative thought had been needed, but these were always subjected to the most searching interrogation before Faraday would commit himself to an opinion. James could see that Faraday's notion of lines of force was far from a vague flight of fancy; it was a serious theory.

Faraday had puzzled hard and long about the way magnets behave. He concluded that a magnet is not just a piece of iron with interesting properties but the centre of a system of invisible curved tentacles, or lines of force, which spread through all space. In Faraday's scheme, magnetic attraction between a north pole and a south pole arises because every tentacle runs from one pole to the other and exerts a pull along its length like a piece of elastic. On the other hand, magnetic repulsion, as between two north poles, comes about because the tentacles push sideways against each other like pieces of compressed rubber. Near the magnet's poles the tentacles are packed closely together and the forces are great; far away the tentacles are sparse and the forces small. One can see why Sir George Airy called the idea 'vague and varying'. But anyone who has seen the beautiful curved patterns made by iron filings sprinkled on a sheet of paper near a magnet can see exactly what Faraday had in mind. The filings become little magnets and are pulled into perfect alignment along the lines of force, each line of filings being kept separate from neighbouring lines by the sideways repulsion.

To explain electrostatic forces between electrically charged bodies, Faraday postulated electric lines of force which behaved in a similar way. And he went further by suggesting that a magnet induces a kind of tension in any nearby loop of metal wire, which will make a current flow if either magnet or wire is moved. He called this the electrotonic state.

To James, Faraday's ideas rang strong and true; all they lacked was numerical expression. If he could find a way to represent lines of force mathematically, he should be able to show that all the known formulae for static electrical and magnetic effects could be derived from them just as well as from the hypothesis of action at a distance. This would confound Faraday's critics and, although it would not itself be a new theory, it might give James a base from which he could develop one.

The present task was to deal with stationary lines of force. This was a limited objective: a complete theory of electricity and magnetism would need to deal also with moving lines, but that could come later. The static problem was essentially geometrical, but it was a more complex geometry than that of Euclid. The curving lines of force filled all space and at every point a force acted with a particular strength along the line that passed through it. This was the geometry of vectors, quantities which vary continuously through space in both magnitude and direction. Although the formal mathematics of vectors was in its infancy some good work had already been done by others and James was able to make use of it. We shall come to that, but first James wanted to get as far as he could by simply following the steps in Faraday's reasoning, giving the lines of force a rigorous quantitative interpretation but using as few mathematical symbols as possible.

But where could one start? Were there any other physical phenomena which behaved something like lines of force and were mathematically amenable? If so, perhaps an approach by analogy might work. Inspiration was at hand. It came from William Thomson, the Glasgow University colleague of cousin Jemima's husband Hugh Blackburn, whom James had first met while he was still at school. Only 7 years older than James, Thomson was already an influential figure and well established as Professor of Natural Philosophy at Glasgow University. While still an undergraduate at Cambridge he had made a remarkable discovery—the equations for the strength and direction of electrostatic force had the same mathematical form as those describing the *rate* and direction of a steady flow of heat through a solid material. It seemed a bizarre association, static force and moving heat, but James saw a chink of light; surely this was an idea worth pursuing. He knew Thomson well by now and wrote announcing his wish to 'poach on your electrical preserves'. Thomson enjoyed the role of mentor and was delighted to agree. Like James, he was more concerned with advancing human knowledge than with building his own reputation, and in any case was by now deeply engaged in other work, including the most exciting technology of the day—the telegraph.

William Thomson's comparison of electrostatic force to heat flow was an inspired insight but did not quite fill the bill. James wanted an analogy that the mind could grasp more readily than the flow of heat. He was also keen, at this early stage, to avoid even the appearance of proposing any particular physical mechanism for lines of force. The analogy he chose was that of an imaginary weightless and incompressible fluid flowing through a porous medium: the streamlines of flow would represent lines of either electric or magnetic force and he could vary the porosity of the medium from place to place to account for the particular electrical or magnetic characteristics of different materials.

Faraday had thought of lines of force as discrete tentacles. James merged them into one continuous essence of tentacle called 'flux'—the higher the density of flux at a point, the stronger the electrical or magnetic force there. The direction of fluid flow at any point corresponded to the direction of the flux and the speed of flow to the flux density. As a device to track the motion of the whole body of swirling fluid, James constructed imaginary tubes for it to flow along. The fluid behaved as though the tubes had real walls, because the lines of flow never crossed one another and the whole system of tubes fitted together, leaving no gaps. The fluid travelled fast where the tubes were narrow and slower where they widened out. Electric and magnetic flux, although stationary, were similarly contained in tubes; and, by analogy, forces were strong where the tubes were narrow and the flux dense, and weak where the tubes were wide and the flux sparse[10].

What made the fluid move was pressure difference. Along each tube the fluid flowed from high pressure to low and the flow at any point was proportional to the pressure gradient there. Correspondingly, flux was caused by differences in electrical potential (voltage) or magnetic potential and the flux density at any point was proportional to the potential gradient, which he called the *intensity* of the field. Points of equal pressure or potential lay on imaginary surfaces which crossed the tubes everywhere at right angles, fitting together like a continuous set of onion skins.

James elaborated the analogy to account for every characteristic of static electricity and magnetism. Positive and negative electrical charges were represented by sources and sinks of fluid, and materials with different susceptibilities to electricity and magnetism by media with different porosity. Electrical conductors were represented by regions of uniform pressure where the fluid was still. And by a separate analogy he found that the flow of the same fluid could also represent an electric current flowing through a conducting material.

It all came together. The fluid analogy not only gave formulae identical to those from the action at a distance hypothesis, it accounted for some electric and magnetic effects which occurred at the boundary between different materials but could not be explained by action at a distance.

The key to it all was that the fluid was incompressible: every cubic centimetre of space always contained the same amount of fluid, no matter how fast the fluid was moving. This automatically led, for example, to the result that electric and magnetic forces between bodies varied inversely as the square of their distance apart—it was simply a matter of geometry[11].

James had vindicated Faraday and turned his 'vague and varying' lines of force into a new and mathematically impeccable concept, the field. So far, he had only dealt separately with static electric and magnetic fields. The difficult problem of working out how the fields interacted when they changed lay ahead, but there was more he could do, even now. It concerned the well-known effect that a moving magnet makes a current flow in any nearby loop of wire. As we have seen, Faraday thought this happened because the magnet, even when stationary, induced a mysterious 'electrotonic state' in the wire, which caused a current as soon as the magnet (or the wire) moved. Odd though it seemed, James felt in his bones that the idea was sound and he set out to find a way to express the electrotonic state mathematically.

For this he had to deviate from his plan to use only pictorial descriptions and simple equations. He needed some power tools and looked into what had already been done in the mathematics of vector quantities. It had been mainly the work of three men. The first was George Green, a Nottinghamshire miller who had taught himself mathematics and eventually managed to get to Cambridge University at the age of 40 but died in 1841, 2 years after gaining a fellowship[12]. The second was none other than William Thomson, who in 1845 found a forgotten paper which Green had written 17 years earlier and saw at once that it was pure gold[13]. He had the paper re-published and started to develop Green's ideas. The third was George Gabriel Stokes, Lucasian Professor of Mathematics at Cambridge, who was a good friend to Thomson and, later, to Maxwell and a valued source of advice and encouragement to both[14].

Making good use of their work, James brought legitimate status to Faraday's electrotonic state by deriving a mathematical expression for it. As usual, it was his intuition that pointed the way. There were two established laws connecting electricity and magnetism. One gave the total magnetic force round an imaginary loop surrounding a wire carrying a given current. The other said how much electric current would be generated in a loop of wire when the magnetic flux passing through the loop increased or decreased at a given rate. These laws appeared to be sound but James felt that they did not quite get to the nub of the matter, because they dealt only with accumulated quantities summed round or through the loop. The only way to get a proper understanding, he thought, would be to look at the intimate relationship between electricity and magnetism in a single small part of space, so he set about re-expressing the laws in what mathematicians call differential form—using vectors at a single point rather than accumulated quantities summed through or round the loop. When he did this he found that one of the vectors exactly fitted Faraday's concept of the electrotonic state: it had no effect when at a uniform and steady value but when it varied over time or space it gave rise to electric or magnetic forces[15]. A success, but to James' mind only a partial one—he had given a mathematical definition but could not think how to interpret the symbols physically, even in terms of an analogy. So the electrotonic state still held on to some of its mystery—for the present.

This was as far as he could go for now. From Faraday's notion of lines of force he had created the *field*, a concept that became the standard pattern for twentieth century physics but was startlingly new to scientists of the time, who were used to thinking of reality in terms of material bodies with passive empty space in between. His system of interlocking forces, fluxes and potentials is exactly what physicists and electrical engineers use today. Even so, he had added little to Faraday's ideas beyond giving them mathematical expression, and the resulting equations, although satisfactory, accounted only for static electrical and magnetic effects. He still had to confront the task of extending the work to include *changing* fields. These appeared to interact in ways quite unlike any other physical phenomenon, and he must have felt he was facing a sheer rock-face. But the field concept gave him a solid base, and by expressing the electrotonic state mathematically he had at least made a toe-hold on the climb.

He called the paper *On Faraday's Lines of Force* and read it to the Cambridge Philosophical Society, taking great care to emphasise that the fluid flow analogy was simply an aid to thought and did not offer even a semblance of a theory as to the nature of either electricity or magnetism[16]. This wise caution derived from his strong philosophical background: analogies can be wonderful as temporary instruments of research but must be kept in their place. He had a charming letter from Faraday:

> I received your paper, and thank you very much for it. I do not venture to thank you for what you have said about 'Lines of Force', because I know you have done it for the interests of philosophical truth; but you must suppose it is work grateful to me, and gives me much encouragement to think on. I was at first almost frightened when I saw such mathematical force made to bear upon the subject, and then wondered to see that the subject stood it so well.[17]

James rarely stopped thinking about electricity and magnetism. When he did he would, after a while, feel 'the electrical state coming on again'. But there was other work to do and it would be 6 years before his next electrical paper appeared. That paper contained one of the greatest scientific discoveries of all time: electromagnetic waves.

By no means all of James' time was spent on research. On top of tutoring duties he set and conducted an examination at Cheltenham College. After gaining his fellowship he lectured on hydrostatics and optics to third-year students. He took pains with these courses and, wherever possible, set up experiments to demonstrate points from the lectures. On one occasion he was saved the trouble: he was showing how to calculate the velocity at which water under pressure would escape through a hole, when a pipe burst in the quadrangle, producing a magnificent jet for all to see. He joined the Ray Club, whose members gave talks in turn on subjects as various as photography and the British administration in India[18]. He also helped to start up a Working Men's College in Cambridge, gave some of the first lectures, and joined in efforts to persuade local businesses to shut early on lecture nights so that workers could attend.

Most of the holidays were spent with his father at Glenlair, but in the summer of 1854 he joined his Cay cousins for a week in the Lake District. He liked them all but had always been particularly fond of Lizzie, who was now a beautiful and very bright girl of 14. They fell in love. It was common in those days for girls to marry at 16 and their thoughts turned in that direction. James was on cloud nine and at the end of the week walked the 50 miles home from Carlisle to Glenlair with a joyful heart. Sadly, they were not to marry. There were worries about consanguinity and they were eventually persuaded by the family to abandon any thought of getting married. It was a deeply wounding experience for both of them, but they got on with their lives and in due course married other people. No letters giving a hint of this affair have survived; clearly they were too painful to keep. We know of it thanks to Professor Francis Everitt, who interviewed Lizzie's daughter when she was in her 90s[19].

In the Christmas vacation of 1854 his father became seriously ill from a lung infection. James' skill as a nurse was put to the test again; he abandoned work on his colour vision paper for several months to take care of the patient. But he did keep up his correspondence, and managed to write in his usual ebullient style; for example:

> ... At present I confine myself to Lucky Nightingale's line of business, except that I have been writing descriptions of Platometers* for measuring plane figures, and privately by letter confuting rash mechanics, who intrude into things

* Devices for measuring areas by tracing around their edges.

they have not got up and suppose their devices will act where they can't.

This is part of a letter to a friend explaining that he would certainly be late for the start of term and might have to miss it altogether[20] He did, indeed, miss the Lent term but, luckily, his father recovered sufficiently for him to return to Cambridge after Easter. It was shortly after this that he heard that he had been elected a Fellow of Trinity, but any notion of settling into a groove was short-lived.

In February 1856 James had a letter from Professor Forbes, letting him know that the chair of Natural Philosophy at Marischal College, Aberdeen, was vacant and suggesting that he apply. Forbes was at pains to point out that he had no influence in the matter; the post was in the gift of the Crown, in the persons of the Lord Advocate and the Home Secretary. James consulted his father and considered whether to put his name forward. If he got the job he would be leaving Cambridge, which was the recognised centre of academic science in Britain, for one of the outposts. On the other hand, he would need to seek a post in the next few years anyway and opportunities did not come up very often. Besides, Cambridge was something of an ivory tower and it would be good to be out in the world. And the short Scottish academic year would allow him to spend more time with his ailing father. He was young and inexperienced for a professorial candidate but that was by no means a bar to selection: William Thomson had been appointed to his Glasgow University chair at 22 and P. G. Tait to his in Belfast at 23.

He decided to apply but at first had no idea how to go about it: he was no careerist. Having found out that testimonials were required from 'swells', he wrote off to all the prominent people he knew who might have something favourable to say. He was himself asked for a testimonial from another candidate, whom he had known at Edinburgh University, and gave it[21]. Among his other rivals was Tait, who wanted to return to Scotland and work in physics: his Belfast post was mathematical.

James' father was buoyed up by the excitement of the venture and by the prospect of seeing more of his son. For a while his health seemed to improve, but it was not to last. They were together at Glenlair during the Easter vacation when John Clerk Maxwell died quite suddenly one morning after James had nursed him through a troubled night.

Now he was alone. His father had been the closest of companions and never far from his thoughts. But sorrow was not the only emotion he felt. There was pride in the love and respect which so many people had felt for his father. And gratitude; he knew how fortunate he was to have had wise and loving parents. He wrote with the news to relations and friends and organised the funeral. And he saw to estate business; knowing how much his father had done to improve the property, he took his new role as Laird very seriously, especially his responsibility for the working men and their families.

Back at Cambridge, James was well into the term's work when he heard that he had been selected for the Aberdeen post. The die was cast. When the bustle of the term was over he packed his papers and his collection of experimental bits and pieces, and with fond memories left Trinity College for Glenlair, where he spent the summer diligently learning the detailed workings of the estate and developing his father's plans, from time to time entertaining relations and Cambridge friends. He also managed to fit in a little experimenting and made a transportable version of his colour box. In November 1856 he set off for Aberdeen.

CHAPTER SIX

SATURN AND STATISTICS

Aberdeen 1856–1860

James took lodgings in the town and prepared to meet his new colleagues. He might have expected to find some of around his own age—Marischal College had, over the years, appointed many young men—but at this time the next youngest professor was 40 and the average age was 55. Perhaps they were glad to have someone young to talk to; at any rate they made their new colleague welcome. In fact, everyone was friendly; James soon found himself dining out more often than at home. The society was congenial, but something was missing. James later wrote to Lewis Campbell: 'No jokes of any kind are understood here. I have not made one for 2 months, and if I feel one coming on I shall bite my tongue'. The contrast with the free badinage of Cambridge must have been sorely felt at times. But he was in good spirits; there was a serious job to be done and he was keen to do it well.

Marischal College, like other Scottish universities, aimed to provide sound, broad and accessible education. Its main business was the 4 year MA degree course, which included as compulsory subjects Greek, Latin, natural history, mathematics, natural philosophy, moral philosophy and logic. Students were mostly from Aberdeen itself and the surrounding countryside. Many were from tradesmen's families; others were sons of farmers, doctors, lawyers, teachers and clergymen. Tradesmen's and farmers' sons rarely took up their fathers' occupations; the most popular careers were medicine, the church, teaching and law. A few graduates went to work as engineers for railway companies abroad. Only one student from Maxwell's time became a recognised scientist —the fine astronomer David Gill.

In those days a new professor was expected to give a formal inaugural lecture to students and staff in which he would set out his intended policy for running the department. This was James' first big speech and he prepared it carefully, drawing on his experiences at Edinburgh and Cambridge, his vast reading, and many discussions with friends on related topics. He made it clear that his objective was not simply to teach science, but rather to use science to teach students to think for themselves and to think straight:

> My duty is to give you the requisite foundation and to allow your thoughts to arrange themselves freely. It is best that every man should be settled in his own mind, and not be led into other men's ways of thinking under the pretence of studying science. By a careful and diligent study of natural laws I trust that we shall at least escape the dangers of vague and desultory modes of thought and acquire a habit of healthy and vigorous thinking which will enable us to recognise error in all the popular forms in which it appears and to seize and hold fast truth whether it be old or new.

And he was most emphatic that experiments must be part of the course:

> I have no reason to believe that the human intellect is able to weave a system of physics out of its own resources without experimental labour. Whenever the attempt has been made it has resulted in an unnatural and self-contradictory mass of rubbish.

Like the other professors, James had complete charge not only of the course of lectures in his department but of the syllabus. This was a weighty responsibility for a newcomer aged 25. Naturally, he already had a plan in his mind of the kind of course he wanted to give but the detail had to be worked out on the job. He was glad to find that his predecessors had also been keen on practical demonstrations, so there was abundant equipment in good working order. Previous courses had been weak in mathematics but that was easily remedied. There was much work to do in preparing the lectures and practical sessions. Like any new teacher, he had the tricky problem of estimating the level at which to approach a topic before he had had time to assess his students' capacity. He prepared every lesson meticulously; to get ready for the optics course, he bought some cods' and bullocks' eyes to refresh his memory and practise dissection. Everything went smoothly and he was off to a good start.

He also agreed to give weekly evening lectures to working men at the Aberdeen Mechanics' Institution. Cambridge had had no Working Men's College until James helped to start one, but in Aberdeen the Mechanics' Institution was already well established. In fact, his predecessors had given lectures there for the past 30 years, a tradition he was pleased to keep up. This gave him a lecturing commitment of 15 hours a week, far from onerous as full-time jobs go, even allowing for preparation time and departmental administration, but a considerable burden for a man also intent on doing front-line research.

For someone so partial to vigorous exercise, Aberdeen was less convenient than Cambridge. There was no gymnasium or bathing shed and the Dee did not have the Cam's rowing facilities. And the winter days were short, so it was important to have a brisk walk at lunchtime. James soon found a colleague to walk with him but after a few weeks his companion fell ill and cried off. At weekends there was the chance to have beautiful coastal walks, and to swim. In a letter to Aunt Jane, James reports his second dip of the season, *in February*, with 'gymnastics on a pole afterwards'! Luckily, no wind of these antics got to the local press, who would have made hay with a 'mad professor' story.

James had little interest in institutional politics but found himself caught up in a conflict which stirred local passions.

Marischal College was not the only university in Aberdeen; there was also King's College. At this time there were only five universities in the whole of Scotland and it is extraordinary that Aberdeen should have had two of them. Some powerful local people were beginning to grudge the expense, and were saying that Marischal and King's should merge, so a Royal Commission was set up to sound out opinions and decide what should be done. Meanwhile, the two establishments coexisted in uneasy rivalry. Naturally sociable, James quickly made friends with some of the younger King's College staff, but found he was swimming against the tide. The prevailing attitude of each university to the other was one of cold politeness; for the most part, professors and their families had no dealings with those from the other place. The debate about a merger rumbled on; as we shall see, it was soon to come to a head.

The new phase of James' life began to take shape. It was an unusual kind of life and in some ways a lonely one. He was a newcomer to the superficially friendly but somewhat closed society of Aberdeen, where he spent the 6 month academic year from November to April. At Glenlair he now lived alone, attending to the estate and enjoying occasional visits from old Edinburgh and Cambridge friends, who had by now scattered far and wide. He also visited aunts, uncles and cousins when he could, but most of the time the only way he could share thoughts with the people to whom he felt closest was by letter. He was greatly saddened when his great friend Pomeroy, whom he had nursed through illness at Cambridge, died bravely in tragic circumstances during the Indian Mutiny. The words James wrote to another friend at this time show how deeply he valued friendship:

> It is in personal union with my friends that I hope to escape the despair which belongs to the contemplation of the outward aspect of things with human eyes. Either be a machine and see nothing but 'phenomena' or else try to be a man, feeling your life interwoven, as it is, with

> many others, and strengthened by them whether in life or death.[1]

These are clearly the words of a man who has not found it easy to master grief and loneliness. Nevertheless, for someone of his buoyant spirit it was a good life. His Aberdeen job was important to him, not so much for the status it conferred as for the chance it gave to help young people gain useful knowledge. He loved Glenlair and there were still many improvements he wanted to make on the estate and in the neighbourhood. Most of all, he was still fascinated by the physical world and determined to find out all he could about it.

It was never his way to concentrate on one research topic to the exclusion of all others but there was one problem that took up most of his free time in 1857—Saturn's rings.

Saturn, with its extraordinary set of vast, flat rings, was the most mysterious object in the universe. How could such a strange structure be stable? Why did the rings not break up, crash down into Saturn, or drift off into space? This problem had been puzzling astronomers for 200 years but it was now getting special attention because St John's College, Cambridge, had chosen it as the topic for their prestigious Adams' Prize.

The Prize had been founded to commemorate John Couch Adams' discovery of the planet Neptune. It may also have been an attempt by the British scientific establishment to atone for its abject performance at the time of the discovery. Adams had spent 4 years doing manual calculations to predict the position of a new planet from small wobbles in the movement of Uranus, then the outermost known planet, but his prediction, made in 1845, was ignored by the Astronomer Royal, Sir George Airy. The following year, the Frenchman Urbain Leverrier independently made a similar prediction. He sent it to the Berlin Observatory, who straightaway trained their telescopes to the spot and found the planet. Perhaps to soothe his conscience, Airy made a retrospective claim on Adams' behalf. Some ill-mannered squabbling followed, from which the only person to emerge with credit was Adams, who had kept a dignified silence. In the end good sense prevailed; Adams and Leverrier were given equal credit. Adams later became Astronomer Royal.

The Adams' Prize was a biennial competition; the Saturn problem had been set in 1855 and entries had to be in by December 1857. The problem was fearsomely difficult. It had defeated many mathematical astronomers; even the great Pierre Simon Laplace, author of the standard work *La mécanique céleste*, could not get far with it. Perhaps the examiners had set the problem more in hope than expectation. They asked under what conditions (if any) the rings would be stable if they were (1) solid, (2) fluid or (3) composed of many separate pieces of matter; and they expected a full mathematical account.

James tackled the solid ring hypothesis first. Laplace had shown that a uniform solid ring would be unstable and had conjectured, but could not prove, that a solid ring *could* be stable if its mass were distributed unevenly. James took it from there. Perhaps thinking 'where on Earth can I start?', he started at the centre of Saturn, forming the equations of motion in terms of the gravitational potential at that point due to the rings. (Potential in gravitation is roughly equivalent to pressure in water systems; difference in potential gives rise to forces.)

In an astonishing sequence of calculations, using mathematical methods which had been known for years but in unheard-of combinations, he showed that a solid ring could not be stable, except in one bizarre arrangement where about four-fifths of its mass was concentrated in one point on the circumference and the rest was evenly distributed. Since telescopes clearly showed that the structure was not lopsided to that extent, the solid ring hypothesis was despatched. James sent his friend Lewis Campbell a progress report, drawing on the Crimean war for his metaphors:

> I have been battering away at Saturn, returning to the charge every now and then. I have effected several breaches in the solid ring and am now splash into the fluid one, amid

> a clash of symbols truly astounding. When I reappear it will be in the dusky ring, which is something like the siege of Sebastopol conducted from a forest of guns 100 miles one way, and 30,000 miles the other, and the shot never to stop, but to go spinning away round in a circle, radius 170,000 miles.

Could fluid rings be stable? This depended on how internal wave motions behaved. Would they stabilise themselves or grow bigger and bigger until the fluid broke up? James used the methods of Fourier to analyse the various types of waves that could occur, and showed that fluid rings would inevitably break up into separate blobs.

He had thus shown, by elimination, that although the rings appear to us as continuous they must consist of many separate bodies orbiting independently. But there was more work to do: the examiners wanted a mathematical analysis of the conditions of stability. A complete analysis of the motion of an indeterminately large number of different-sized objects was clearly impossible, but to get an idea of what could happen James took the special case of a single ring of equally spaced particles.

He showed that such a ring would vibrate in four different ways, and that as long as its average density was low enough compared with that of Saturn the system would be stable. When he considered two such rings, one inside the other, he found that some arrangements were stable but others were not: for certain ratios of the radii the vibrations would build up and destroy the rings. This was as far as he could go with calculation but he recognised that there would be collisions between the particles —a type of friction—and predicted that this would cause the inner rings to move inwards and the outer ones outwards, possibly on a very long time-scale.

James was awarded the Adams' Prize. In fact, his was the only entry. This boosted rather than diminished his kudos because it demonstrated the difficulty of the task; no one else had got far enough to make it worth sending in an entry. The Astronomer

Royal, Sir George Airy, was not, as we have seen, the most reliable judge of scientific merit but he was on safe ground when he declared James' essay to be 'One of the most remarkable applications of Mathematics to Physics that I have ever seen'. The work had been a Herculean labour. In fact it was a triumph of determination as much as creativity; the mathematics was so intricate that errors had crept in at every stage, and much of the time was taken up in painstakingly rooting them out. In all it was a marvellous demonstration of vision, intuition, skill and sheer doggedness and it earned James recognition by Britain's top physicists; he was now treated as an equal by such men as George Gabriel Stokes and William Thomson.

Interestingly, no-one since Maxwell has been able to take our understanding of the rings much further. But flypast pictures from Voyager 1 and Voyager 2 in the early 1980s showed them to have exactly the type of structure that he predicted. Although the essay had won the prize, James spent a lot of time over the next 2 years developing it and trying to make it more intelligible to general readers before publishing it in 1859[2].

To demonstrate some of the kinds of wave motion that can exist in the rings, James designed a hand-cranked mechanical model and had it made by a local craftsman, John Ramage. When the handle was turned, little ivory balls mounted on a wooden ring could vibrate in two different modes. He said it was 'for the edification of sensible image worshippers'. This was probably a dig at William Thomson, who used to say that the test of whether or not we understand a subject is 'Can we make a mechanical model of it?'. The model is now kept in the Cavendish Laboratory in Cambridge, together with a beautiful 'dynamical top', also made by Ramage, which James designed to demonstrate the dynamics of a rotating body in illustration of a short paper on the subject. Clearly James was himself an admirer, if not a worshipper, of 'sensible images'. The dynamical top was a great success as a teaching aid: James had several copies made for friends in various educational establishments and it became a commercial product which stayed in demand until the 1890s.

He took the top with him when visiting Cambridge to collect his M.A. and showed it to friends at an evening party in his room. They left it spinning and one of them was astounded to see it still going round when he called to get James out of bed in the morning. James had seen him coming, started the top and hopped back under the blankets.

Saturn had, for the time being, almost ousted James' other research interests. But with the great labour of the Prize essay out of the way (it weighed 12 ounces), he turned with some relief to optics. He took his colour vision work further, using an improved design of colour box splendidly built by the invaluable Ramage and an ingenious new method of colour matching.

The old method was to find out by direct comparison what mixture of the three primary colours matched the fourth spectrum colour being investigated. Instead, he now mixed the colour under investigation with *two* of the three primaries and found out what combination of these gave a match with natural white light. By already knowing what combination of all three primaries made white, and using a little simple algebra, he could convert the results into the usual form. This method was simpler to operate and made for more consistent matching.

It also provided a neat new solution to the same problem he had faced when experimenting with the colour top—his primary colours inevitably failed to correspond exactly to the characteristics of the eye's three receptors, and so he could not produce all colours by direct mixing. His earlier solution for the awkward colours had been to put a negative quantity of one primary into the mix by combining it with the colour to be matched, rather than with the other two primaries. But the new method gave a simple, direct match for all colours; sometimes this implicitly involved a negative amount of one primary but the negative sign appeared only when the relevant colour equation had been recast into the usual form.

He also put forward a new approach to the theory of optical instruments, defining the instrument by what goes into it and what comes out (what engineers call the 'black box' approach), rather than by the details of the internal reflections and refractions. He simply worked out the geometrical relations between the spaces occupied by the object and the image—in modern engineering terms, the transfer function between the instrument's input and its output. Optics was a highly developed branch of science and yet no-one before Maxwell had thought of doing this.

But the most famous work he did at Aberdeen, containing a truly fundamental scientific discovery, was on a topic he had not previously explored: the kinetic theory of gases. We shall come to that, but meanwhile other things were happening.

James had become a favourite with the College Principal, the Rev. Daniel Dewar, and his family. He often visited their house and was asked to join them on a family holiday. He and Professor Dewar's daughter, Katherine Mary, enjoyed being together and became more and more attracted to one another. This was, as far as we know, James' first romantic attachment since the doomed affair with his cousin Lizzie. He proposed and Katherine accepted; they became engaged in February 1858 and were married in Aberdeen in June.

Lewis Campbell came up from Hampshire to be best man. He and his new wife were the Maxwells' first guests at Glenlair. James had been best man at their wedding in Brighton a few weeks earlier. It was a joyful time. So much is clear from James' letters to friends: the metaphors fly even more exuberantly than usual. Here he writes to Campbell in March to tell him of the engagement and the approximate date of the wedding, and to invite him and Mrs Campbell to Glenlair afterwards:

> When we had done with the eclipse today, the next calculation was about the conjunction. The rough approximations bring it out early in June ...
>
> The first part of May I shall be busy at home. The second part I may go to Cambridge, to London, to Brighton, as may be devised. After which we concentrate our two selves at Aberdeen by the principle of concerted tactics. This done, we

steal a march, and throw our forces into the happy valley, which we shall occupy without fear, and we only await your signals to be ready to welcome reinforcements from Brighton ...

It was an unusual match. Katherine was 34, 7 years older than James, and may well have almost given up hope or thought of marriage before James came along. Both had known a measure of loneliness, and perhaps felt a joyful relief at having found a lifetime companion. James said as much in a poem:

Trust me spring is very near,
  All the buds are swelling;
All the glory of the year
  In those buds is dwelling.

What the open buds reveal
  Tells us—life is flowing;
What the buds, still shut, conceal,
  We shall end in knowing.

Long I lingered in the bud
  Doubting of the season,
Winter's cold had chilled my blood—
  I was ripe for treason

Now no more I doubt or wait,
  All my fears are vanished
Summer's coming dear, though late,
  Fogs and frosts are banished.

They both looked forward to being together at Glenlair. James had accompanied his proposal with a poem that invites Katherine to share the place that meant so much to him:

Will you come along with me,
  In the fresh spring tide,
My comforter to be
  Through the world so wide?

Will you come and learn the ways
A student spends his days
On the bonny bonny braes
  Of our ain burnside.

. . .

And the life we then shall lead
  In the fresh spring tide
Will make thee mine indeed,
  Though the world be wide.
No stranger's blame or praise
Shall turn us from the ways
That brought us happy days
  On our ain burnside.[3]

Their honeymoon was a month of enjoying 'sun, wind, and streams' at Glenlair before James got back to work. Katherine helped where she could, particularly with the colour vision experiments, using the colour box. They each obtained matches of a range of pure spectrum colours with mixtures of red, green and blue and James included both sets of observations in his published results[4]. Plotted on a chromaticity diagram, they are very close to the standard results used today, which were published by the Commission Internationale d'Eclairage in 1931.

In April 1859, James read a paper by the German physicist Rudolf Clausius, which captured his imagination at once. It was about diffusion in gases—for example, the speed with which the smell from a bottle of perfume will spread through air when the bottle is opened. The eighteenth century Swiss physicist and mathematician Daniel Bernoulli had proposed what later became known as the kinetic theory of gases: that gases consist of great numbers of molecules moving in all directions, that their impact on a surface causes the gas pressure that we feel, and that what we experience as heat is simply the kinetic energy of their motion. Others had developed the theory further and by the mid-nineteenth century it was able to offer an explanation for most of the gas laws on pressure, volume and temperature which had been found by experiment.

But there was a difficulty over the speed of diffusion. For the theory to explain pressure at normal temperatures, the molecules would have to move very fast—several hundred metres per second. Why then do smells spread relatively slowly? Clausius proposed that each molecule undergoes an enormous number of collisions, so that it is forever changing direction—to carry a smell across a room it would actually have to travel several kilometres. The sheer scale of the process is astounding. James put it this way:

> If you go at 17 miles per minute and take a totally new course 1,700,000,000 times in a second, where will you be in an hour?[5]

In his calculations, Clausius had assumed that at a given temperature all molecules of any one kind travel at the same speed. He knew this could not be exactly true but could not think what else to do. Nor, at first, could James. The problem of representing the motion of gas molecules mathematically was a bit like that he had faced with Saturn's rings; and then he had settled for second best —calculating the results only for a simple special case. But now he had an inspiration which, at a stroke, opened the way to huge advances in our understanding of how the world works.

The standard mathematical methods, derived from Newton's laws of motion, were of little use on their own because of the impossibility of analysing so many molecular motions, one by one. James saw that what was needed was a way of representing many motions in a single equation, a *statistical* law. He derived one, now known as the Maxwell distribution of molecular velocities. It said nothing about individual molecules but gave the proportion which had velocities within any given range.

The sheer audacity of the way he arrived at this law is astounding. It comes out in a few lines, with no reference to collisions; in fact there seems to be no physics in it at all. The argument goes something like this:

1. In a gas at uniform pressure and at a steady temperature, composed of molecules of one type, let the velocity of each molecule be represented by components x, y and z along three arbitrarily selected axes at right angles to each other. The total speed, s, of any particular molecule, irrespective of direction, will then be equal to the square root of the sums of the squares of its values of x, y and z (simply Pythagoras' theorem extended to three dimensions and applied to the addition of velocities).
2. As the axes are perpendicular to each other, the number of molecules with any particular value of one velocity component, say x, will not depend on the numbers which have particular values of the other components y and z. But it will depend on how many molecules have particular values of the total speed s[6].
3. Since there is no reason for molecules to move faster in any one direction than another, the form of the velocity distribution is the same along each axis.

These three statements imply a particular kind of mathematical relationship, which is easily solved, giving a formula for the statistical distribution of velocities along any of the three axes. Since the axes are arbitrary the velocities in any other direction also have this distribution.

This was the first-ever statistical law in physics—the Maxwell distribution of molecular velocities. The distribution turned out to have the bell-shaped form that was already familiar to statisticians and is now generally called the normal distribution. The top of the bell-curve corresponded to a velocity of zero and its sides were symmetrical in the positive and negative directions. Its shape varied with temperature: the hotter the gas, the flatter and wider the bell. The average velocity in any particular direction was always zero, whatever the temperature, but the average *speed*, irrespective of direction, was greater the higher the temperature.

And from the statistical distribution of velocities, it was a simple matter to derive the distribution of speeds.

He had made a discovery of the first magnitude. It opened up an entirely new approach to physics, which led to statistical mechanics, to a proper understanding of thermodynamics and to the use of probability distributions in quantum mechanics. If he had done nothing else, this breakthrough would have been enough to put him among the world's great scientists.

The key to the argument was the assumption, embodied in statement 2, that the three components of velocity are statistically independent. This was pure intuition. James felt that it must be true, although he conceded that the assumption 'may appear precarious'. Years later the formula was verified in experiments, showing that his intuition was correct.

Like so many of James' ideas, this one sprang from analogy. For years, physicists had used statistical methods to allow for errors in their experimental observations; they knew that errors in measurement tended to follow statistical laws. Social scientists, too, had used such methods to study characteristics of populations. What had occurred to no-one before Maxwell was that statistical laws could also apply to *physical processes*. James recalled reading, about 9 years earlier, an account of the work of Adolphe Quetelet, the Belgian statistician, which included a simple derivation of the formula for errors which underlies the method of least squares, a way of making the best estimate from a scattered set of observations[7]. This gave just the analogy he needed. In hindsight it seems so simple; anyone could have picked up the least squares formula and applied it to gases. But to make the connection it needed, to repeat Robert Millikan's words, 'one of the most penetrating intellects of all time'.

At this time, no-one *knew* that gases consist of molecules, still less whether it was their motion that determined their physical properties. Even among physicists who favoured the idea of molecules, most still held to Newton's conjecture that static repulsion between them was the cause of pressure. Indeed, James had been taught the static theory at Edinburgh, but his intuition drew him strongly to the kinetic theory. It had by now become a plausible contender because it could explain physical laws which had already been found by experiment. But James went further: he used the kinetic theory to predict a new law. Now there could be a proper test: if experiments showed the prediction to be false, then the theory would be disproved, but if they showed it to be true, the theory would be greatly strengthened.

The new law that he predicted seemed to defy common sense. It was that the viscosity of a gas—the internal frictional that causes drag on a body moved through it—is independent of its pressure. One might expect a more compressed gas to exert a greater drag; even James was surprised at first that the theory said otherwise. But further thought showed that, at higher pressure, the effect on a moving body of being surrounded by more molecules is exactly counteracted by the screening effect they provide: each molecule travels, on average, a shorter distance before it collides with another one. A few years later, James and Katherine themselves did the experiment which showed the prediction to be correct.

This was James' first venture into gas theory. It was a magnificent piece of work but by no means devoid of flaws. He made a second prediction—that viscosity should increase as the square root of absolute temperature—but, as we shall see, when he later tested this by experiment it turned out to be wrong. He made mistakes when trying to prove a relation which he was intuitively convinced was true: that the energy in a gas is equally divided between linear and rotational energy. His intuition was right—the principle is an important one now called the equipartition principle—but his proof was faulty. There were more mistakes in his derivation of equations for heat conduction. And he made some arithmetical errors: he was out by a factor of about 8000 when calculating the ratio of the thermal conductivity of copper to that of air because he had forgotten to convert kilograms to pounds and hours to seconds!

For all its faults, the work drew admiration, particularly from continental scientists. Clausius was prompted by it to make another attempt at some of the intractable problems, at the same time pointing out James' errors. Gustav Kirchhoff, who is best remembered as the inventor of spectroscopy, said, 'He is a genius, but one has to check his calculations'. Even these admirers failed to see the full significance of James' introduction of statistical methods into physics. But there was one man who did. He was at this time a teenage student in Vienna and did not see James' paper until about 5 years later, but was then so inspired by it that he spent much of a long and distinguished career developing the subject further; his name was Ludwig Boltzmann. During the 1860s and 1870s he and James took turns in breaking new ground, and Boltzmann continued after James died, putting the science of thermodynamics on a rigorous statistical basis. Although they never thought of themselves as such, they were a splendid partnership. It is fitting that their names are now immutably joined in the Maxwell–Boltzmann distribution of molecular energies.

James presented his results when the British Association for the Advancement of Science met in Aberdeen in September 1859, and published the paper in two parts the following year[8]. The meeting was a big event, attended by Prince Albert, and a number of interested citizens, including James, had raised the money for a fine new building to house it. Much later, the building became the town Music Hall and during the early 1900s a firm of advocates had the job of paying small dividends to the original subscribers. Not being able to trace one of them, they eventually put an advertisement in a local newspaper, asking anyone who knew the whereabouts of a Mr James Clerk Maxwell to get in touch. A school inspector who had made a study of Maxwell's time in the town went along and asked if they had really never heard of Professor Clerk Maxwell, the most famous man ever to walk the streets of Aberdeen. No, they hadn't. After the inspector had given a fulsome account of Maxwell's accomplishments, the advocate said 'That's very interesting. We put the advertisement in because for years we have been sending dividends to Mr James Clerk Maxwell, Marischal College, and they have always been returned "not known" '.

What of James' classes? Had he succeeded as a teacher? The nearest short answer one can give is 'no' and 'yes'. For all his talents, he never mastered the technical part of teaching. He would prepare a lesson beautifully, do fine for a time while he stuck to his script, and then fly into analogies and metaphors which were intended to help the students but more often than not mystified them. He was not expert on the blackboard, where he made algebraic slips which took time to find and correct. And yet the students liked him and some found him truly inspiring. This report is from George Reith, who became Moderator of the Church of Scotland and father of Lord Reith, the first Governor of the British Broadcasting Corporation:

> But much more notable [than the other professors] there was Clerk Maxwell, a rare scholar and scientist as the world came to know afterwards; a noble-souled Christian gentleman with a refined delicacy of character that bound his class to him in a devotion which his remarkably meagre qualities as a teacher could not undo.

And this one from David Gill, who became Director of the Royal Observatory, Cape of Good Hope:

> After the lectures, Clerk Maxwell used to remain in the lecture room for hours, with three or four of us who desired to ask questions or discuss any points suggested by himself or ourselves, and would show us models of apparatus he had contrived and was experimenting with at the time, such as his precessional top, colour box, etc. These were hours of the purest delight to me.
>
> ... to those who could catch a few of the sparks that flashed as he thought aloud at the blackboard in lecture, or when he twinkled with wit or suggestion in after lecture conversation, Maxwell was supreme as an inspiration.

It seems paradoxical that such a fine scientific writer should be so lacking in basic teaching skill, especially as he believed fervently in the value of good education and had firm ideas on the principles to be followed. The principal difficulty lay in oral expression. It did not arise when he gave a formal speech and stuck closely to his text, nor in ordinary conversation, where, in congenial company, he could give free rein to his imagination. But in the lecture room he seemed to be caught between the two modes. Appreciating that people learn in different ways, he may have tried too hard to bring in helpful illustrations and analogies, confusing his audience with a welter of rapidly changing images. In Lewis Campbell's words, 'the spirit of indirectness and paradox, though he was aware of the dangers, would often take possession of him against his will'.

And perhaps he was too much of an idealist. All good teachers aim, as he did, to teach people to think for themselves, but most also recognise that all some students want is to gain a second-hand smattering of the subject so that they can pass exams, and make a specific effort to help them succeed in this limited ambition. Maxwell never did.

He did, however, do his utmost to help any student who truly wanted to learn. Students could take only two books at a time from the library but professors could take any number, and sometimes took a book for a friend. James used to take out books for his students, and when challenged by colleagues replied that the students were his friends. And his talks to working men were remembered long after he left Aberdeen. A farmer recalled how the professor had stood one of them on an insulating mat and 'pumpit him fu' o' electricity' so that his hair stood on end.

The debate about merging the two universities had moved on. The Royal Commission had decided that they *would* merge and the issue became whether there should be 'union', a common management of otherwise little-changed faculties, or 'fusion', a complete amalgamation, which would halve the number of professors. The fusionists gained the day and the new University of Aberdeen was set to get under way at the beginning of the academic year 1860–1861. There would be only one chair in natural philosophy, and James' rival for the post was David Thomson, his opposite number at King's College. Thomson was also Sub-Principal and Secretary of the College and an astute negotiator who had earned the nickname 'Crafty'. James was clearly up against it, especially as to discharge him was the cheaper option—he would get no pension, not having served the requisite 10 years. Set against these factors was James' achievement in research, but only a few people had any idea of its importance and none of them lived in Aberdeen. Thomson was chosen and James was made redundant.

Exactly at this time, James Forbes' post as professor of natural philosophy at Edinburgh University became vacant—Forbes had been ill and was leaving to become Principal of St Andrews University. This was an appealing possibility. James would be succeeding his great friend and mentor. And in Edinburgh he would be among friends and relations and relatively close to Glenlair. He applied and so did his friend P. G. Tait, who was still at Belfast. This time the Aberdeen order was reversed and Tait was preferred.

Out of one job and turned down for another. But he was not long in the wilderness. King's College, London, also wanted a professor of natural philosophy. James entered his name and was selected.

There was plenty to do in the meantime. Besides preparing his great paper on gas theory for publication, he wrote another, on elastic spheres, and sent a report on his colour experiments to the Royal Society of London. Shortly afterwards he heard that the Society had recognised this work by awarding him the Rumford Medal, its highest award for physics. There was estate business to see to and an important local project was to raise funds for the endowment of a new church at Corsock, just north of Glenlair.

During the summer he went to a horse fair and bought a handsome bay pony for Katherine. Soon after returning he became violently ill, with a high fever. It was smallpox, almost certainly contracted at the fair, and it nearly killed him. James was in no doubt that it was Katherine's devoted nursing that saved his life.

Once on the mend, he broke in Charlie, the new pony, riding side-saddle with a carpet to take the place of a lady's riding habit. In October 1860, after an eventful year, James and Katherine packed and set off for London.

CHAPTER SEVEN

SPINNING CELLS

London 1860–1862

The Maxwells rented a house in the smart new residential district of Kensington[1]. This gave James a vigorous 4 mile walk to work on fine days, with the alternative of a horse-drawn bus ride. Nearby was the great green space of Kensington Gardens and Hyde Park—a fine place to stroll and to ride. Katherine's pony, Charlie, also made the long railway journey down from Glenlair and, once he was settled into stables from which James could hire a horse, they rode most afternoons. At the top of the house was a big attic, just the place for James' experimental paraphernalia. Neighbours across the way were alarmed at first to see the two of them spending hours in this room, peering into what looked like a coffin, but it turned out to be James' new and bigger colour box, about 8 feet long, which they had put near the window to get the best light.

King's College is in The Strand by the north bank of the river Thames. It had been founded in 1828 as an Anglican alternative to the non-sectarian University College, a mile to the north, which was itself intended as an alternative to the strictly Church of England universities of Oxford and Cambridge. King's was a *modern* university. From the outset it strove to give young people an education to fit them for working life in a rapidly developing world. Unlike the traditional fare provided by Cambridge and Aberdeen, its courses were much like those given at today's universities. It gave classes in new subjects like chemistry, physics,

botany, economics and geography, and ran purpose-built courses in law, medicine and engineering.

There was, of course, an inaugural lecture to be given. At the age of 29, James was already becoming an old hand at these. As he had done at Aberdeen, he stressed that he wanted above all to help people learn to think for themselves:

> In this class, I hope you will learn not merely results, or formulae applicable to cases that may possibly occur in our practice afterwards, but the principles on which those formulae depend, and without which the formulae are mere mental rubbish.
>
> I know the tendency of the human mind is to do anything rather than think. But mental labour is not thought, and those who have with labour acquired the habit of application, often find it much easier to get up a formula than to master a principle.

He finished the lecture with what turned out to be an extraordinarily prophetic statement:

> Last of all we have the Electrical and Magnetic sciences, which treat of certain phenomena of attraction, heat, light and chemical action, depending on conditions of matter, of which we have as yet only a partial and provisional knowledge. An immense mass of facts has been collected and these have been reduced to order, and expressed as the results of a number of experimental laws, but the form under which these laws are ultimately to appear as deduced from central principles is as yet uncertain. The present generation has no right to complain of the great discoveries already made, as if they left no room for further enterprise. They have only given science a wider boundary, and we have not only to reduce to order the regions already conquered, but to keep up constant operations on a continually increasing scale.

James was attacking the widespread misconception that there was little left to do in science beyond measuring nature's characteristics to more places of decimals. Just the kind of rhetoric one might expect from a keen new professor. But within 4 years he was to turn rhetoric into accomplishment by creating a theory which masterfully brought everything together and, at the same time, extended the boundaries of science into undreamt-of regions.

As at Aberdeen, the post was a demanding one for someone who was also engaged in top-level research. The lecturing load was a little lighter than at Aberdeen but the terms took up 8 months of the year rather than 6. There were also weekly evening talks to artisans—at King's these were part of the professor's official duties. The course James took over was well designed but he improved it further by increasing the practical work and introducing the latest discoveries, which were often his own. The pattern served King's well—100 years later it was still considered a very good course. He tried to make examination questions more interesting by couching them in terms of everyday experiences, and insisted that the question papers should be printed rather than lithographed, to make sure all copies were legible.

Among James' professorial colleagues was Charles Wheatstone, who is familiar to physics students as the supposed inventor of the Wheatstone bridge—a type of circuit used to measure electrical resistance. Curiously, Wheatstone did not invent this bridge, even though he was a prolific inventor who created the English concertina and, like William Thomson, earned a fortune from patents on telegraph devices. Whatever spurious kudos Wheatstone gained from the bridge is balanced by the genuine credit he lost when one of his outstanding inventions became well known under someone else's name, the Playfair cipher[2]. He and James clearly had interests in common and it seems odd that they had little, if any, contact. The oddity seems to lie mainly in Wheatstone's relationship with the university. He had been in post 26 years but for the last 25 of those had spent his time on research and inventions and given no lectures. He played little part in College life and by the time James arrived was not even drawing a salary.

Living in London gave James the chance to attend lectures and discussions at the Royal Society and, more particularly, the Royal Institution, where Faraday had built on Davy's foundation by establishing a celebrated tradition of popular lectures. He and James had built up a scholarly comradeship by letter but it was a delight for James to meet the scientist he admired above all others. Faraday still attended some lectures but now rarely gave them. He was in his 70s and suffering from failing memory, but he and James took pleasure in one another's company and it is pleasing for us to picture them together—two modest and genial men from different backgrounds but sharing a passionate interest, whose combined endeavours brought about a metamorphosis in science and technology.

James was invited to give a lecture at the Royal Institution on his work on colour vision in May 1861. Rather than just talk about the principles, he wanted to give the audience a visual demonstration that any colour could be made by mixing the three primaries. The colour box was no good for this purpose because only one person could use it at a time, and the colour top was too small for people in the back seats to see clearly.

But there was another possibility. The basic techniques of black and white photography were known and it was possible to project a photograph on to a screen. Could he make a *colour* photograph? He would simply need to take three photographs of the same object, through red, green and blue filters in turn, and then project them simultaneously on to the screen using the same filters. There was a problem: photographic plates of the time were sensitive to light at the blue end of the spectrum but hardly, if at all, sensitive to light at the red end. Still, it was worth a try. Thomas Sutton, a colleague at King's, was an expert photographer and keen to help. They took three pictures of a tartan ribbon, developed the plates, and it worked beautifully. The Royal Institution audience saw the world's first colour photograph.

Amazingly, all attempts at emulating James' feat failed: it was many years before the next colour photograph appeared. How did he do it? The mystery was solved about 100 years later by a team at Kodak Research Laboratories.

The experiment should never have worked because the plates that Maxwell and Sutton used were, in fact, completely insensitive to red light. There had been a bizarre chain of favourable coincidences. The red dye in the ribbon happened to reflect some ultra-violet light as well as the red, and the solution used by Sutton as a red filter happened to have a pass-band in the same ultra-violet region. Moreover, although the emulsion used on the plates was not at all sensitive to red, it happened to be sensitive to ultra-violet. So the parts of the picture which appeared red had actually been obtained with ultra-violet light, well beyond the range of the human eye! Lucky Maxwell. But perhaps he made his own luck. It was a rule with him never to dissuade a man from trying an experiment, no matter how slim the prospect of success, because he might find something entirely unexpected.

Three weeks after his colour show, and one week before his 30th birthday, James was elected to the Royal Society, in recognition of his work on Saturn's rings and colour vision. It must have given him some gratification to be welcomed formally into the top rank of British physicists—although he was nowhere near as well known as Thomson or Stokes—but the event seems to have barely registered in the Maxwell household. Perhaps he had the private wistful thought that his father would have enjoyed it.

At the time he joined King's College James had published only one paper on electricity and magnetism, and that had been 5 years before. But the subject was never far from his mind and ideas had been steadily brewing. He believed strongly in the power of subconscious thought to generate insights. As a student he had expressed this theory in a poem:

> There are powers and thoughts within us, that we know not till they rise
> Through the stream of conscious action from where Self in secret lies.

> But where will and sense are silent, by the thoughts that come and go
> We may trace the rocks and eddies in the hidden depths below.[3]

He later put the same idea in a letter to a friend:

> I believe there is a department of the mind conducted independently of consciousness, where things are fermented and decocted, so that when they are run off they come clear.[4]

In his Cambridge paper *On Faraday's Lines of Force* he had found a way of representing the lines of force mathematically as continuous fields, and had made a start towards forming a set of equations governing the way electrical and magnetic fields interact with one another. This was unfinished business and he now felt ready to make a serious attempt to settle it. He had made progress so far by using the analogy of a swirling body of incompressible fluid—the pressure in the fluid corresponded to electric or magnetic potential and the direction and speed of flow represented the direction and strength of either an electric or a magnetic field. By extending the imagery, so that, for example, sources and sinks of fluid represented electrically charged surfaces, he had been able to derive all the important formulae for static electricity and magnetism. He had also managed to bring steady electric currents and their effects into the scheme by using the fluid analogy in a different role to represent the flow of electricity.

The analogy had served well but could take him no further because it worked only when electrical and magnetic fields were static and electric currents steady. As soon as anything changed, the fields acted in a way that was nothing like the smooth flow of a fluid; in fact their behaviour was completely different from that of any known physical process. So to go further he had to find a new approach.

Two courses seemed to be open. One was to desert Faraday and fields, and assume that all effects result from action at a distance between magnetic poles and electrical charges or currents. This was the approach taken by Siméon-Denis Poisson and André-Marie Ampère, who had derived the original formulae for static fields and steady currents which James had re-derived by the field approach. It was also the basis of an attempt at a complete theory by Wilhelm Weber, which was mathematically elegant and offered an explanation for most of the known effects. But Weber had made a critical assumption—that the force between two electrical charges depends not only on their distance apart but also on their relative velocity and acceleration along the straight line joining them. James respected Weber's work but his intuition bridled at this assumption and, more generally, at the whole action at a distance concept.

He therefore chose the second route, which was to go beyond geometrical analogy and make an imaginary mechanical *model* of the combined electromagnetic field—a mechanism that would behave like the real field. If he could devise a suitable model, the equations governing its operation would also apply to the real field.

As we have seen, all the known experimental results in electricity and magnetism could be attributed to four types of effect; to gain the day, James' model would have to account for all of them:

1. Forces between electrical charges: unlike charges attract; like charges repel, both with a force inversely proportional to the square of the distance between the charges.
2. Forces between magnetic poles: unlike poles attract; like poles repel, both with a force inversely proportional to the square of the distance between them; poles always occur in north/south pairs[5].
3. A current in a wire creates a circular magnetic field around the wire, its direction depending on that of the current.
4. A changing total magnetic field, or flux, through a loop of wire induces a current in the wire, its direction depending on whether the flux is increasing or decreasing.

And it would need to do so precisely, so that all the established formulae involving electric charge and current, magnetic pole strength, distances and so on could be derived from the model, together with any new formulae.

James began with effect 2, magnetic forces. For his model he needed to envisage a medium filling all space which would account for magnetic attraction and repulsion. To do this, it would need to develop tension along magnetic lines of force and exert pressure at right angles to them—the stronger the field, the greater the tension and the pressure. And to serve its purpose as a model the imaginary medium would have to be built from components which bore some resemblance to everyday objects.

It seemed an impossible task, but James' idea was amazingly simple. Suppose all space were filled by tiny close-packed spherical cells of very low but finite density, and that these cells could rotate. When a cell rotated, centrifugal force would make it tend to expand around the middle and contract along the spin axis, just as the earth's rotation causes it to expand at the equator and flatten at the poles. Each spinning cell would try to expand around the middle but its neighbours would press back, resisting the expansion. If all the cells in a neighbourhood spun in the same direction, each would push outwards against the others; they would collectively exert a *pressure* at right angles to their axes of spin.

Along the axes of spin the opposite would happen. The cells would be trying to contract in this direction and there would be a *tension*. So if the spin axes were aligned along lines in space, these lines would behave like Faraday's lines of force, exerting an attraction along their length and a repulsion sideways. The faster the cells spun, the greater would be the attractive force along the lines and the repulsive force at right angles to them—in other words, the stronger the magnetic field.

So the field would act along the spin axes of the cells. But which way? Magnetic force is conventionally defined as acting from north pole to south pole. James built an extra convention into his scheme: the sense of the field would depend on which way the cells were spinning—it would be in the direction a right-handed screw would move if it rotated the same way; if the cells reversed their spin, the field would reverse too.

But if the cells occupied all space, why were they not apparent? And how could they exist in the same space as ordinary matter? James was not put off by such awkward questions. It was, after all, only a model. The cells' mass density could be so low as to offer no perceptible obstruction to ordinary matter. As long as they had *some* mass and rotated fast enough they would generate the necessary forces.

The scheme did not yet explain how different materials could have different magnetic characteristics. For example, iron and nickel had a high magnetic susceptibility—they could be readily magnetised—whereas other substances, like wood, seemed to be even less receptive to magnetism than empty space. James solved this problem with his customary sureness of touch. Where cells occupied the same space as an ordinary substance their behaviour would be modified according to the magnetic susceptibility of the substance. The modification was equivalent, in mechanical terms, to a change in the mass density of the cells. In iron, for example, they would become much more dense than in air or empty space, thereby increasing the centrifugal forces, and hence the magnetic flux density, for a given rate of spin.

Here was the basis of a model. The spin axes of the cells gave the direction of the magnetic field at any point in space: their density and rate of spin determined its strength, and the model provided exactly the right equations for effect 2, magnetic forces in static situations.

So far so good. But there were two problems. First, what set the cells in motion? And second, the cells along one line would be spinning in the same direction as those in neighbouring lines, so that where two surfaces made contact they would be moving in opposite directions, rubbing awkwardly against one another. Amazingly, James solved both problems with a single stroke.

To avoid the cells rubbing against one another, he tried putting even smaller spherical particles between the cells. They would act like ball bearings, or like the 'idle wheels' engineers put between two gear wheels which need to rotate in the same direction. The idea seemed crazy but James persevered and suddenly things began to fall into place. Suppose the little idle wheels were particles of electricity. In the presence of an electromotive force they would tend to move along the channels between the cells, constituting an electric current, and it would be this movement that set the cells spinning.

But everyone knew that currents could flow only in substances which were conductors, like metals. In insulators like glass or mica, or in empty space, there could be no currents. So James proposed a second way in which the behaviour of the cells would be modified according to the type of substance which shared their space. In an insulator the cells, or perhaps local groups of cells, would hold on to their little particles so that they could rotate but not move bodily. But in a good conductor like a copper wire the particles could move bodily with very little restriction and a current would flow. In general, the lower the electrical resistance of the substance, the more freely the particles could move.

An essential feature of James' little particles was that they had rolling contact with the cells—there was no sliding. Where the magnetic field was uniform the particles would just rotate, along with the cells. But if the particles in a conductor moved bodily without rotating, they would cause the cells on either side of the current to spin in opposite directions, exactly the condition to create a circular magnetic field around a current-carrying wire—effect 3. If the particles rotated *and* moved, the circular magnetic field due to their movement would be superimposed on the linear one due to their rotation.

So, by this extraordinary assemblage of tiny spinning cells interspersed with even smaller 'idle wheel' particles, James had succeeded in explaining two of the four main properties of electricity and magnetism. A highly satisfactory start, but there was much more to do. The next task was to explain effect 4: a changing magnetic flux through a loop of wire induces a current in the wire. James chose to explain an equivalent effect—that

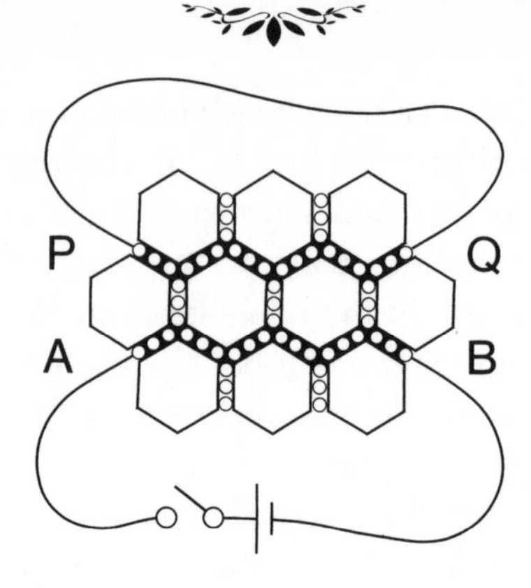

Figure 2a. Switch open

- All cells and idle wheels stationary
- No currents
- No magnetic fields

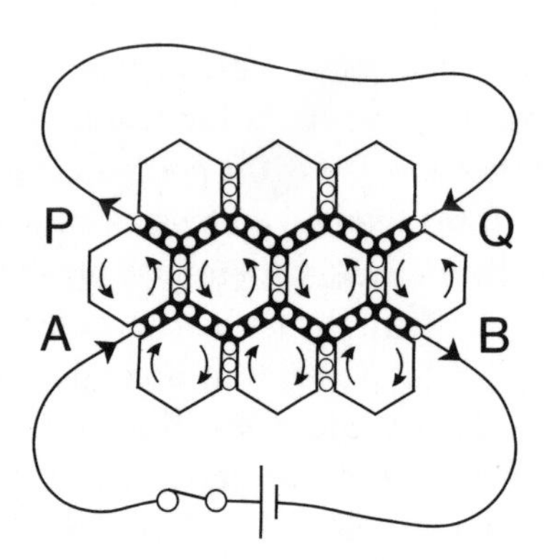

Figure 2b. Switch first closed

- AB current flows from left to right
- PQ current flows from right to left
- Cells below AB rotate clockwise, causing a magnetic field pointing away from the viewer
- Cells between AB and PQ rotate anticlockwise, causing a magnetic field pointing towards the viewer (in three dimensions, a circular field envelopes AB)
- Cells above PQ still stationary

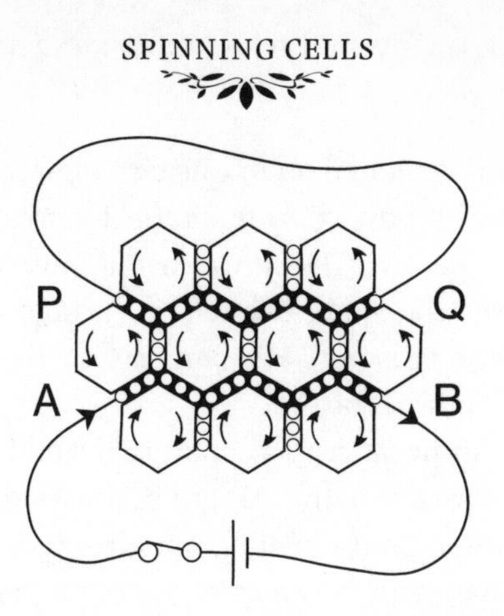

Figure 2c. Shortly after switch closed

- PQ current slows, then stops
- Cells above PQ start to rotate anticlockwise, and by the time the current stops are rotating at the same rate as those in the row below PQ

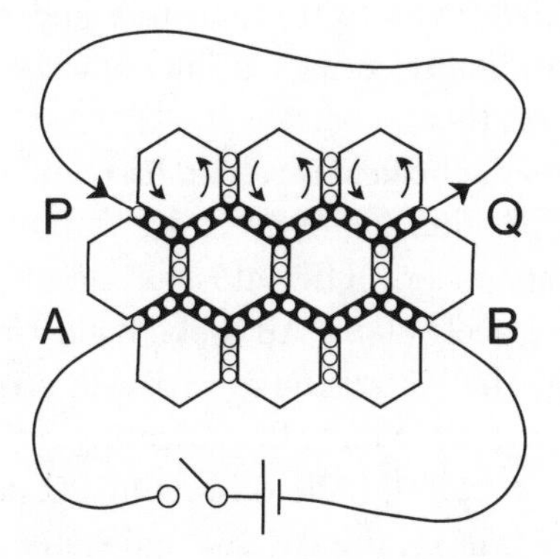

Figure 2d. Switch opened again

- AB current stops
- Cells in rows above and below AB stop rotating
- PQ current flows from left to right
- The current will slow, then stop; the situation will then be as in Figure 2a

when a current is switched on in one circuit, it induces a pulse of current in a nearby but separate circuit by creating a magnetic field that links the two. He drew a diagram to illustrate his argument, giving the spherical cells a hexagonal cross-section 'purely for artistic reasons'. We can see it, slightly adapted for our purpose, in Figures 2a–d.

The diagram shows a cross-section of a small region of space. The idle wheel particles along AB are in a wire which is part of a circuit with a battery and a switch, initially open. Those along PQ are in another wire which is part of a separate circuit having no battery or switch. The idle wheels along AB and PQ are free to move because they are in conductors, but others in the neighbourhood are in a non-conducting material and can only rotate in their fixed positions. AB and PQ are, of course, impossibly thin wires and impossibly close together, but this is to just keep the diagram compact; the argument James produced would apply equally well to normal-sized and normally spaced wires containing many rows of idle wheels and cells. The argument runs like this.

Suppose the magnetic field is zero at first, and the switch open, so that all the cells and idle wheels are stationary (Figure 2a). When the battery is brought into the circuit by closing the switch, the idle wheels along AB move bodily from left to right without rotating. This causes the rows of cells on either side of AB to rotate in opposite directions, thus creating a circular magnetic field around the wire. The idle wheels in PQ are now pinched between rotating cells on the AB side and stationary ones on the other, so they start to rotate (clockwise) and also to move from right to left, the opposite direction from those in AB (Figure 2b).

But the circuit containing the wire along PQ has some resistance (all circuits do), so the idle wheels there, after their initial surge, will slow down, causing the cells above PQ to begin rotating anticlockwise. Soon, the sideways movement of the idle wheels will stop, although they will continue to rotate. By this time the cells above PQ will be rotating at the same rate as those in the row below PQ (Figure 2c).

When the switch is opened again, disconnecting the battery, the idle wheels along AB stop moving and the rows of cells on either side of AB stop rotating. The idle wheels in PQ are now pinched between stationary cells on the AB side and rotating ones on the other, so they start to move from left to right, the same direction as the original AB current (Figure 2d).

Once again the resistance of the circuit containing PQ causes the idle wheels there to slow down. This time, when their sideways movement stops they will be not be rotating; we are back to the state represented in Figure 2a.

Thus, switching on a steady current in AB induces a pulse of current in PQ in the opposite direction and switching the current off induces another pulse in PQ, this time in the same direction as the original current. More generally, any *change* of current in the AB circuit induces a current in the separate PQ circuit through the changing magnetic field that links them. Equivalently, any change in the amount of magnetic flux passing through a loop of wire induces a current in the loop—effect 4 is explained. If the battery in the AB circuit were replaced by an a.c. generator, the alternating AB current would induce an alternating current in PQ. This is exactly the way transformers work in our electrical power supply systems.

And here, at last, was a mechanical analogy for Faraday's electrotonic state. It was the effect at any point in the field of the angular momentum of the spinning cells. Like a flywheel, the cells would act as a store of energy, reacting with a counterforce to resist any change in their rotation; this took the form of an electromotive force which would drive a current if a conductor was present.

James had now explained three of the four effects. He had not yet found a way of using the model to account for effect 1, forces between electric charges, commonly called electrostatic forces. But he wrote up the results with full mathematical rigour in a paper called *On Physical Lines of Force*, which was published in the *Philosophical Magazine* in monthly instalments: Part 1 appeared in March 1861 and Part 2 was spread over April and May. Not wanting to be misunderstood, he was at pains to point out that his bizarre arrangement of whirling cells and idle wheels was merely a *model*:

> The conception of a particle having its motion connected with that of a vortex* by perfect rolling contact may appear somewhat awkward. I do not bring it forward as a mode of connexion existing in nature, or even as that which I would willingly assent to as an electrical hypothesis. It is, however, a mode of connexion which is mechanically conceivable, and easily investigated, and it serves to bring out the actual mechanical connexions between the known electromagnetic phenomena; so that I venture to say that any one who understands the provisional and temporary nature of this hypothesis, will find himself rather helped than hindered by it in his search after the true interpretation of the phenomena.

He had failed to achieve a full theory and it was with a feeling of disappointment that he and Katherine left London to spend the summer vacation at Glenlair. But it was good to get back to the easy rhythm of country life, with its concerns over crops, plantations and farm animals, and to the fresh Galloway air. He had not planned to do any serious work on electricity and magnetism during the summer and took no reference books. But his thoughts ran on and an idea began to crystallise.

It seemed a small idea at first. The material making up his little cells had to transmit the twisting forces internally so that each cell would rotate as a body. To do this without dissipating energy the material needed to have a degree of springiness, or elasticity. The idea grew. Could this elasticity be the source of the forces between electric charges which he had so far been unable to explain?

* In Parts I and II of the paper Maxwell called his rotating elements 'vortices'. In later parts he used the alternative term, 'cells'. For simplicity here we call them cells from the outset.

In conductors currents could flow because the electrical particles, the idle wheels, were free to move bodily in response to an electromotive force. Continuous currents could not flow in insulators because the particles were bound to their neighbouring cells. But *elastic* cells would distort, allowing the particles to move a short distance. The distortion in the cells would cause a restoring force, like a spring. The particles would move until the spring-back force balanced the electromotive force.

So, for example, if a battery were connected by metal wires across two metal plates separated by an insulating material, there would be a small *displacement* of the electrical particles in the insulator away from one plate and towards the other. This small movement was, in effect, a brief electric current. The movement of electricity would be the same all round the circuit so that in the wires, where particles were not bound to cells, the same brief current would flow. This would result in a surplus of particles on the surface of one plate and a shortage on the surface of the other, so one plate would become positively charged and the other negatively. The distorted cells in the insulating material between the charged metal plates would act like a wound-up spring, exerting a mechanical force of attraction between them. So the elasticity of the cells explained the force between the charged plates.

Even when the battery was disconnected the spring would stay wound up, storing energy. If the plates were then connected by a metal wire, the spring's energy would be released: a brief current would flow in the wire, the charges on the plates would fall back to zero and the cells and idle wheels would return to their rest positions.

Following his earlier thinking, James proposed that the elasticity, or spring-stiffness, of the cells would be modified if they were sharing their space with ordinary matter, and that the degree of modification would depend on the type of matter. The higher the electrical susceptibility of the substance, the softer the spring and the greater the electrical displacement for a given electromotive force. For example, filling the space between the metal plates with mica rather than air would soften the spring and increase the amount of charge on the plates for a given voltage across them.

He wrote up the mathematics and everything fitted together. James had shown how the electrical and magnetic forces which we experience could have their seat not in physical objects like magnets and wires but in energy stored in the space between and around the bodies. Electrostatic energy was potential energy, like that of a spring; magnetic energy was rotational, like that in a flywheel, and both could exist in empty space. And these two forms of energy were immutably linked: a change in one was always accompanied by a change in the other. The model demonstrated how they acted together to produce all known electromagnetic phenomena.

A triumph. But there was more. The model predicted two extraordinary and entirely *new* physical phenomena which took physics into undreamt-of territory.

One was that there could be electric currents anywhere, even in perfect insulators or in empty space. According to the model, as we have seen, there would be a little twitch of current whenever an electromotive force was first applied to an insulator, because the electrical idle wheels would move slightly before being halted by the spring-back force of their parent cells. In the model all space is filled with cells, so these twitches of current would occur even in empty space.

This new type of current would arise whenever the electric field changed. Its value, at any point, would depend on the rate of change of the electric field at that point. In fact, it was simply the rate of displacement of electricity due to the small movement of the particles. James asserted that it was in every way equivalent to an ordinary current. He gave it the name '*displacement current*'.

The equations governing electrical and magnetic effects had hitherto just dealt with the ordinary conduction current. In James' new theory, the displacement current had to be added in. When this was done the system of equations was transformed from a motley collection into a beautifully coherent set. This was not immediately evident, however, even to James; he had seen something even more interesting.

All materials that have elasticity transmit waves. James' all-pervading collection of cells was elastic, so it must be capable of carrying waves. In an insulating material, or in empty space, a twitch in one row of idle wheels would be transmitted via their parent cells to the surrounding rows of idle wheels, then to the rows surrounding them, and so on. Because the cells have inertia they would not transmit the motion instantly but only after a short delay—the twitch would spread out as a ripple. So any change in the electric field would send a wave through all space.

What is more, any twitch in a row of idle wheels would make the neighbouring cells turn a bit and so generate a twitch in the magnetic field along the cells' axes of spin. All changes in the electric field would therefore be accompanied by corresponding changes in the magnetic field, and vice versa. The waves would transmit changes in both fields; they were *electromagnetic* waves.

What kind of waves were they? Waves in the sea or along a rope are called 'transverse' because the individual particles of sea or rope move at right angles to the direction of the wave. Waves like sound are called 'longitudinal' or 'compression' waves because the particles move back and forth along the same line as the wave. James' electromagnetic waves were clearly *transverse* because the changing electric and magnetic fields were both at right angles to the direction of the wave.

James felt he was on the verge of a great discovery. Light waves were known to be transverse. Could light consist of waves of the kind his model predicted? The speed of light was known with reasonable accuracy from experiments and astronomical observations. It was also well known that the speed of waves in any elastic medium is given by the square root of the ratio of the medium's elasticity to its density. In the model, the elasticity of the cells controlled the electrostatic (spring-back) forces and their density the magnetic (centrifugal) forces. James' calculations showed that the spring stiffness of his cells in empty space was not completely determined: it could vary over a factor of three[6]. But if he set it at the lowest value in this range—equivalent to assuming that the cell material was a hypothetically perfect solid—a remarkable result would follow. The wave speed in empty space, or in air, would then be exactly equal to the ratio of the electromagnetic and electrostatic units of electric charge*. It seemed impossible that such a simple and natural result could be wrong, so James confidently set the elasticity of his cells to fit it.

He now had a very simple formula for the speed of his waves. To check their speed against that of light he first needed to look up the result of an experiment by Wilhelm Weber and his colleague Rudolf Kohlrausch. They had measured the ratio of the *electrodynamic* and electrostatic units of charge; electrodynamic units are closely related to electromagnetic ones, so James would easily be able to convert their result to give the value for the ratio he needed. He also needed to look up the exact values for the experimentally measured speed of light. But he had brought no reference books; this would have to wait until he got back to London in October. The summer passed in a glow of anticipation.

He had left for Glenlair disappointed at having failed to produce a complete theory of electromagnetism. He returned to London not only with a complete theory but with two entirely new predictions, displacement current and waves. Moreover, the waves might turn out to include light. He eagerly looked up Weber and Kohlrausch's experimental result and from it worked the speed of his predicted waves. In empty space or air they would travel at 310,740 kilometres per second. Armand-Hippolyte-Louis Fizeau had measured the speed of light in air as 314,850 kilometres per second.

* The ratio is the number of electrostatic units in one electromagnetic unit. The electromagnetic unit is bigger because it takes a bigger charge to generate a given force by electromagnetic action than by electrostatics. The ratio has the dimensions of a velocity because electrostatic force depends only on the charge but electromagnetic force depends additionally on its velocity.

Plate 1. Frances Clerk Maxwell (née Cay) with her son, James. Portrait by Sir William Dyce, whose sister was married to Frances' brother. Courtesy of Birmingham Museums and Art Gallery

Plate 2. John Clerk Maxwell, James' father. After a portrait by Sir John Watson Gordon. Courtesy of Sir Robert Maxwell Clerk of Penicuik, Bt

Plate 3. Maxwell's Aunt Jane (left) and his mother, Frances, as girls. Portrait by their mother, Elizabeth Cay. Courtesy of the James Clerk Maxwell Foundation

Plate 4. Drawing by Maxwell, aged 14. Courtesy of the Master and Fellows of Trinity College, Cambridge

Plate 5. The Edinburgh Academy in 1840. Courtesy of The Edinburgh Academy

Plate 6. The Old Quadrangle at Edinburgh University, as it was when Maxwell was a student there. Courtesy of the University of Edinburgh

Plate 7. Maxwell's colour top. The inner and outer parts each carry overlapping coloured paper discs which can be adjusted until both parts appear the same colour when the top is spun. Courtesy of the Cavendish Laboratory, Cambridge

Plate 8. Maxwell, aged 24, holding the colour top. Courtesy of the Master and Fellows of Trinity College, Cambridge

Plate 9. Maxwell's model to show the motion of the satellites which make up Saturn's rings. When the handle is cranked, the little ivory balls demonstrate two kinds of wave motion. Courtesy of the Cavendish Laboratory, Cambridge

Plate 10. Maxwell's dynamical top, a teaching aid made from solid brass to illustrate the principles of angular momentum. Its balance, or imbalance, can be adjusted using the nine screws. The disc on the spindle carries coloured sectors which combine to appear grey when the top is spinning smoothly but break into their separate colours when it is disturbed. Courtesy of the Cavendish Laboratory, Cambridge

Plate 11. Marischal College, Aberdeen. Drawing by Samuel Read, reprinted from the *Illustrated London News* of 1 October 1859. Courtesy of the University of Aberdeen

Plate 12. The opening of the British Association meeting in Aberdeen. Prince Albert is making the inaugural address. Drawing by Samuel Read, reprinted from the *Illustrated London News* of 1 October 1859. Courtesy of the University of Aberdeen

Plate 13. Charles Hope Cay, Maxwell's cousin. Courtesy of Clifton College

Plate 14. William Dyce Cay, Maxwell's cousin and Charles' elder brother. Courtesy of the Institution of Civil Engineers

Plate 15. Maxwell, aged about 30. Courtesy of the Master and Fellows of Trinity College, Cambridge

Plate 16. Katherine Clerk Maxwell (née Dewar), James' wife. Courtesy of the Master and Fellows of Trinity College, Cambridge

Plate 17. Peter Guthrie Tait. Portrait by Sir George Reid. Courtesy of the Royal Society of Edinburgh

Plate 18. Lord Kelvin (William Thomson) in 1902. Photograph by Annan of Glasgow. Courtesy of the University of Glasgow

Plate 19. Glenlair, after enlargement. Courtesy of Sam Callander

Plate 20. Remains of Glenlair, photographed in 1991. Courtesy of Dr David Summers

Plate 21. Maxwell in his mid-40s. Engraving by G. J. Stodart from a photograph by Fergus of Greenock. Courtesy of Edinburgh City Libraries

The correspondence seemed too close for coincidence, even allowing for a possible error of a few percent in each of the experimental results. Light must consist of electromagnetic waves. Some of the greatest leaps in science have come when two sets of apparently different phenomena are explained by a single new theory. This was one such leap: at a stroke, he had united the old science of optics with the much newer one of electromagnetism.

James had not expected to extend his paper *On Physical Lines of Force* beyond Parts 1 and 2 but now he set about writing Part 3, which covered electrostatics, displacement current and waves, and Part 4, which used his model to explain why polarised light waves change their plane of vibration when they pass through a strong magnetic field—an effect discovered experimentally by Faraday. Even for one with the calmest of temperaments it must have been an exhilarating time. The two further parts of the paper were published early in 1862. In Part 3, James announced:

> We can scarcely avoid the inference that light consists in the transverse undulations of the same medium which is the cause of electrical and magnetic phenomena.

The idea of a medium, an 'aether' pervading all space, was far from new. Physicists of the day believed an aether of some kind was necessary to transmit light waves, so one might have expected ready acceptance of James' application of the principle to electricity and magnetism. But there were misgivings; the reaction of his friend Cecil Monro was typical:

> The coincidence between the observed velocity of light and your calculated velocity of a transverse vibration in your medium seems a brilliant result. But I must say I think a few such results are needed before you can get people to think that every time an electric current is produced a little file of particles is squeezed along between two rows of wheels.

The difficulty lay deep in the scientific thinking of the time. People believed that all physical phenomena resulted from mechanical action and that all would be clear to us if, and only if, we could discover the *true* mechanisms. With a century and a half of hindsight we can see the spinning cell model as a crucial bridge between old and new ideas—built from old materials but paving the way for a completely new type of theory, one which admits that we may never understand the detailed workings of nature. One cannot blame James' contemporaries for seeing things differently. To many of them the model was simply an ingenious but flawed attempt to portray the true mechanism, for which the search would continue.

James himself was not entirely content with the model, but for different reasons. He wanted to free the theory if possible from all speculative assumptions about the actual mechanism by which electromagnetism works. He was to achieve this wish 2 years later by taking an entirely new approach. Scientific historians now look upon his spinning cells paper as one of the most remarkable ever written but hold the one that followed to be greater still.

CHAPTER EIGHT

THE BEAUTIFUL EQUATIONS

London 1862–1865

There were other kinds of work to be done. James and Katherine steadily accumulated more data on colour vision using the box which neighbours had mistaken for a coffin. All new guests at their house soon found themselves looking into the strange wooden box, trying to match colours. This way, the Maxwells were able to carry out the first-ever survey of the amount of variation in colour perception among both normal-sighted and colour-blind people. The box gave good results but the work was laborious: the lenses and prisms had to be kept in exact alignment, and for each observation the widths of three slits had to be adjusted by successive approximation until a match had been found. And the work had to be fitted in when more pressing occupations allowed. Nevertheless, they recorded about 200 observations each year.

In his Aberdeen paper *Illustrations of the Dynamical Theory of Gases*, James had made the bold prediction that the viscosity, or internal friction, of a gas is independent of the pressure. It was important to carry out an experiment; if the prediction was borne out, this would greatly strengthen the theory that gases were composed of molecules whose motion causes the properties we can measure, like pressure and temperature. The experiment would be tricky, and so far no-one had done it. James resolved to try.

The choice of gas was easy—air would serve the purpose very well. Measuring its viscosity would be more difficult. One way would be to time the rate at which it damped down the swings of a pendulum. James decided to use a torsional pendulum, sealed inside a big glass case so that the pressure of the air in which it swung could be controlled by a pump.

The 'bob' of the pendulum was a stack of three glass discs about ten inches in diameter which were spaced about an inch apart and suspended by a steel wire so they could rotate together. The wire was about 5 feet long and the whole apparatus, which stood on a tripod, was much taller than a man. A magnet was fixed to the bottom of the wire so that an external electromagnet could be used to set the pendulum swinging around its vertical axis. Fixed glass plates were interleaved with the rotating discs so that the viscosity of the air in the narrow spaces between the fixed and the moving glass surfaces would damp the swings of the pendulum. A small mirror was attached to the wire so that the swings could be tracked using a reflected light beam which projected a moving spot on to a screen. If the prediction was correct, the pendulum swings would die down at the same rate whatever the pressure of air inside the glass case.

He had the apparatus built and brought to the attic at the top of the house which served as a laboratory. The course of the experiment did not run smoothly. First the pressure seals failed, then the glass case violently imploded; but they persevered and eventually got a set of readings which looked promising.

Encouraged, James set about testing the second prediction from his Aberdeen paper: that viscosity should increase as the square root of absolute temperature. For this they put the big glass case inside a metal jacket into which water at various temperatures or steam could be passed. To insulate the jacket they wrapped it in their spare blankets and put a big feather cushion on the top. It was still hard to keep the apparatus at a constant temperature, so they had to try to control the temperature of the whole room. Lewis Campbell reports that for the high temperature readings Katherine stoked a large fire and for the low they carried up great quantities of ice. But this time there were no technical hitches and they took a good set of readings.

James took the two sets of data with him to Glenlair for the summer vacation, but forgot his log tables so he had to do all the calculations by hand. Tenacity was rewarded: the first set of results magnificently verified his prediction that viscosity was constant over a wide range of pressures. But the second set of readings brought a shock. Viscosity certainly did *not* vary as the square root of absolute temperature; in fact it seemed to come closer to varying directly with temperature[1].

Some serious reassessment was called for. The molecular theory had provided one correct prediction and one false one. Did the two predictions depend on the theory in different ways? Indeed they did. The pressure law was more robust: it would hold for any kind of molecules. The temperature law, on the other hand, depended on a specific assumption about the molecules: that they behaved like rough-surfaced billiard balls, bouncing off each other and transferring spin. The fault must lie with this assumption.

There were other loose ends. Rudolf Clausius had found errors in James' derivation of the law that the kinetic energy in a gas is divided equally between linear and rotational energy. No-one had yet found a satisfactory proof of this law, but James felt sure that it was correct and that a proof would be found. There was, however, a much more disturbing problem.

The law made a prediction that disagreed with a well-established experimental result. It predicted that the ratio between the specific heat* of air at constant pressure and that at constant volume should follow a simple formula involving the number of independent modes of molecular motion. For James' molecules the formula gave a value of 4/3 or 1.333, but experiments on several common gases had shown it to be 1.408. This was a faith-shaking result and for a while it made James

* The amount of energy needed to raise the temperature of one mass unit of the gas by one degree.

doubt the molecular hypothesis altogether. He had weathered those doubts but the apparent contradiction between theory and practice was still a serious worry. For the moment he had reached an impasse. As was his way, he despatched the outstanding problems to 'the department of the mind conducted independently of consciousness'.

Meanwhile the young Viennese student Ludwig Boltzmann, who had started to puzzle about the same problems, belatedly discovered James' Aberdeen paper. With intuition akin to James' own, he quickly saw that the statistical approach was the key to understanding the way that gases behaved and started to think along similar lines, preparing the ground for what was to be a splendid cross-fertilisation of ideas.

James was becoming heavily involved in an entirely different kind of work, not in the least glamorous but nonetheless demanding and crucially important—the development of a coherent set of units of measurement for electricity and magnetism. The new science was bedevilled by a chaotic rag-bag of units and this was already beginning to hamper the progress of technology. Someone had to sort out the mess. The British Association for the Advancement of Science had asked James to lead a small team to make a start in bringing things to order. His colleagues were two other Scotsmen: Fleeming Jenkin, who was also an old boy of the Edinburgh Academy, and Balfour Stewart.

The seeds of the problem were historical. Magnetism and static electricity had been known for centuries but were regarded as separate phenomena. Some enlightened scientists had suspected a link but it was only in the nineteenth century that proof came.

There were three key events. In 1799 the Italian Count Alessandro Volta invented the voltaic pile, or battery, which provided a source of *continuous* electric current: previously it had only been possible to store electricity in such devices as the Leyden jar, which released all its charge in one burst. Volta had not set out to produce currents; he merely wanted to show that his friend Luigi Galvani was wrong. Galvani believed that the electricity by which he had made dead frogs' legs twitch came from animal tissue but Volta thought it was generated by chemical action between different metals in the circuit. His first pile, or battery, built from repeated layers of silver, damp pasteboard and zinc, was intended simply to prove he was right. It did indeed prove the point but the battery soon took on a life of its own and people started to use currents for such things as electro-plating. Curiously, the name they first gave to the phenomenon of continuous electric currents was not 'voltism' but 'galvanism'.

Now that scientists had electric currents, the link between electricity and magnetism was waiting to be found. It only needed someone to put a magnetic compass near a current-carrying wire and notice that the needle was deflected. Amazingly, 21 years passed before Hans-Christian Oersted switched on a current while lecturing to a class and happened to glance at a compass lying on the bench. He was astonished to see the needle jerk; the link was proved. News of Oersted's discovery spread fast. Within a few months Ampère had worked out how to use magnetism to measure currents, and by the following year Faraday had made a primitive electric motor.

If electric currents produce magnetism, surely magnetism should produce electric currents. Scientists tried many experiments but found no currents. It was a further 11 years before Faraday discovered that to make a current flow in a wire loop you needed to *change* the amount of magnetic flux passing through it: the faster the change, the bigger the current—the same principle is used today to generate the electrical power we use in our homes, offices and factories[2].

So magnetism, static electricity and current electricity were inextricably bound together. But because of the way the science had grown up, they were measured in different ways. The task of setting up a coherent set of units was formidable. The very connectedness of electricity and magnetism meant that quite a lot of units were needed and that some were fairly complex. An example is the unit of self-inductance. Any loop of wire carrying a current generates a magnetic field which acts through the loop, and whenever the current changes the consequent change in magnetic flux induces an electromotive force in the wire which is proportional to the rate of change of current, and opposes the change. The number of units of electromotive force generated in the loop when the current changes at a rate of one unit per second is called the self-inductance of the loop; our unit for it is the henry, named after Faraday's American contemporary Joseph Henry, who designed the world's first powerful electromagnet and invented the electromagnetic relay, which made long-distance telegraphy practical.

No-one had yet made a systematic review of all the various quantities in electricity and magnetism, and how they should be measured. James took on this task and, with Fleeming Jenkin's help, wrote a paper for the British Association which included recommendations for a complete system of units. These were later adopted almost unchanged as the first internationally accepted system of units, which became known, misleadingly, as the Gaussian system (Gauss's contribution was certainly less than Maxwell's and probably less than those of Thomson and Weber).

In fact, confusion over units was not confined to electricity and magnetism. When two people spoke of a quantity like 'force' or 'power' you could not be sure that they meant the same thing. James saw a prime opportunity to straighten out the muddle. He went beyond his brief for the paper and proposed a systematic way of defining all physical quantities in terms of mass, length and time, symbolised by the letters **M**, **L** and **T**. For example, velocity was defined as $\mathbf{L}/\mathbf{T}$, acceleration $\mathbf{L}/\mathbf{T}^2$, and force $\mathbf{ML}/\mathbf{T}^2$, since, by Newton's second law, force = mass × acceleration. His method is used in exactly this form today. Called dimensional analysis, it seems to us so simple and so natural a part of all physical science that almost nobody wonders who first thought of it.

For the key units in electricity and magnetism, it was becoming important to have physical *standards* to which all measurements could, in principle, be referred. The reference would, in practice, be made by using transportable copies of the standard. Most urgently of all, the burgeoning telegraph industry needed a standard of electrical resistance so that enforceable contracts could be drawn up for the supply of serviceable cables. The unit of resistance was named after Georg Simon Ohm, the German mathematics teacher who had proposed Ohm's law: that the current flowing in an element of a circuit is proportional to the potential difference, or voltage, between its ends. The resistance of the element is numerically equal to the voltage needed to make one unit of current flow in it.

James and his colleagues set out to produce a standard of electrical resistance. The task was difficult because the method would have to use only measurements involving mass, length and time. To rely on measurements of electrical or magnetic quantities would defeat the purpose because no physical standards existed for them. But resistance is the ratio of voltage to current, so how on earth do you measure it without measuring either a voltage or a current? Such is the ingenuity of physicists that several ways were known. They chose one suggested by William Thomson.

The idea was to mount a circular wire coil on a vertical axis and spin it rapidly in the earth's magnetic field. An electromotive force, or voltage, would thereby be induced in the coil; this would cause a current to flow and the amount of current would depend on the coil's resistance. The current in the coil would, in turn, create its own magnetic field which would vary in strength as the coil went round but would always act towards either the east or the west, depending on which way the coil was spun. A small magnet, delicately suspended at the middle of the coil, would swing back and forth but eventually settle at the angle where the deflecting effect of the coil's field was balanced by the restraining effect of the earth's field. The beauty of this arrangement was that the deflection was independent of the strength of the earth's field—whatever that strength, it contributed equally to the deflecting and restraining forces on the magnet so that their ratio was the same. Thus the magnet's angle of deflection from magnetic north would depend only on the resistance of the coil, along with known factors such as the dimensions of the coil and the speed of rotation.

Almost so, anyway. The small magnet's own field would contribute to the current in the coil and hence to the coil's field. This complicated the mathematics but did not pose a serious problem, as the relative strengths of the magnet's and the earth's fields could be measured separately.

What about the fact that the coil's field varied as the coil rotated; would the magnet not wobble in sympathy? No, it would not. Provided the coil was spun rapidly, its field would vary so much faster than the magnet's natural rate of oscillation that the magnet would, in effect, respond only to the average value of the coil's field.

The theory was elegant but putting it into practice was not easy. Their revolving coil had many turns of copper wire wound on a circular former about 10 inches in diameter and was cranked by hand via a pulley mechanism which had a governor, designed by Jenkin, to hold the speed steady. They measured the speed by timing each 100 revolutions, and to measure the deflection of the magnet they used a scale with a built-in telescope. Each run took about 9 minutes and had to be repeated when anything went wrong. Mechanical breakdowns took their toll and readings were upset by the magnetic effect of iron ships passing up or down the Thames. The work was, perforce, sporadic because James and his colleagues were busy men, but after months of patient endeavour they had a satisfactory set of readings and an accurate value for the resistance of the coil. When the spinning was done they needed to unwind the copper coil to measure its length precisely. Even this was tricky because the wire had to be straightened without being stretched. Luckily there was a nearby gallery in the College museum where the wire could be gently straightened by pushing it into convenient grooves between the floorboards.

But copper was an unsuitable material for a transportable standard because its resistance changed appreciably with temperature, and the wire they had used was in any case too fragile and unwieldy to serve the purpose. So the final operation was to use it in an electrical balance to set the resistance of a robustly built coil of German silver wire. James and his colleagues had given the world its first standard of electrical resistance[3]. And the work brought another benefit. During his long cranking sessions, with the governor automatically regulating the coil's rate of spin, James' thoughts turned to the theory of such devices. As we shall see, he later wrote a pioneering paper on the subject.

James was alert to all new developments in physics and engineering, and kept his students up to date. To calculate stresses in frameworks, such as girder bridges, he gave them the latest methods of William Rankine, professor of civil engineering at Glasgow University. The calculations could be laborious, so James thought of a dramatic way to simplify them. The trick was to draw 'reciprocal diagrams' in which lines converging to a point in the real structure became polygons in the diagram and vice versa. To give the method a sound base, he derived a set of general theorems on the properties of these diagrams when applied to two- and three-dimensional structures. His paper, *On Reciprocal Figures and Diagrams of Forces*, was the first of a series he wrote on this topic. The method was to become common practice in engineering design, and a related technique was later employed to determine the shape of crystal lattices by X-ray and electron crystallography.

It was at this time, busy as he was with experiments and College business, that Maxwell produced a paper which will remain forever one of the finest of all man's scientific accomplishments, *A Dynamical Theory of the Electromagnetic Field*. Its boldness, originality and vision are breathtaking.

The work had been many years in gestation. Most creative scientists, even the most prolific and versatile, produce one theory per subject. When that theory has run its course they move on to another topic, or stop inventing. Maxwell was unique in the way he could return to a topic and imbue it with new life by taking an entirely fresh approach. To the end of his life there was not one subject in which his well of inventiveness showed signs of exhaustion. With each new insight he would strengthen the foundations of the subject and trim away any expendable superstructure. In his first paper on electromagnetism he had used the analogy of fluid flow to describe static electric and magnetic effects. In the second he had invented a mechanical model of rotating cells and idle wheels to explain all known electromagnetic effects and to predict two new ones, displacement current and waves. Even the most enlightened of his contemporaries thought that the next step should be to refine the model, to try to find the *true* mechanism. But perhaps he was already sensing that the ultimate mechanisms of nature may be beyond our powers of comprehension. He decided to put the model on one side and build the theory afresh, using only the principles of dynamics: the mathematical laws which govern matter and motion.

Much of the mathematics he had developed in earlier papers was still applicable, in particular the way of representing electric and magnetic fields at any point in space at any time. But to derive the equations of the combined electromagnetic field independently of his spinning cell model he needed something else.

It sometimes happens that mathematical methods conceived in the abstract turn out later to be so well suited to a particular application that they might have been written especially for it. When he was wrestling with the problems of general relativity, Albert Einstein came across the tensor calculus, invented 50 years earlier by Curbastro Gregorio Ricci and Tullio Levi-Civita, and saw that it was exactly what he needed[4]. James enlisted a method that had been created in the mid-eighteenth century by Joseph-Louis Lagrange.

Lagrange was a consummate mathematician with a penchant for analysis and for the orderly assembly and solution of equations. Unlike James, he distrusted geometry—his masterpiece on dynamics, the *Mécanique analytique*, did not contain a single diagram. He had devised a way of reducing the equations of motion of any mechanical system to the minimum number and lining them up in standard form like soldiers on parade. For each 'degree of freedom'—each independent component of motion—a differential equation gave the rate of that motion in terms of its momentum and its influence on the kinetic energy of the whole system[5].

For James, the keynote of Lagrange's method was that it treated the system being analysed like a 'black box'—if you knew the inputs and could specify the system's general characteristics you could calculate the outputs *without knowledge of the internal mechanism*. He put it more picturesquely:

> In an ordinary belfry, each bell has one rope which comes down through a hole in the floor to the bellringer's room. But suppose that each rope, instead of acting on one bell, contributes to the motion of many pieces of machinery, and that the motion of each piece is determined not by the motion of one rope alone, but by that of several, and suppose, further, that all this machinery is silent and utterly unknown to the men at the ropes, who can only see as far as the holes above them.

This was just what he needed. Nature's detailed mechanism could remain secret, like the machinery in the belfry. As long as it obeyed the laws of dynamics, he should be able to derive the equations of the electromagnetic field without the need for any kind of model.

The task was formidable; James had to extend Lagrange's method from mechanical to electromagnetic systems. This was new and hazardous ground, but he was well prepared. From study of Faraday and from his own work he had built up a strong intuition for the way electricity and magnetism were bound together and how their processes were, in some ways, similar to mechanical ones.

His cardinal principle was that electromagnetic fields, even in empty space, hold *energy* which is in every way equivalent to mechanical energy. Electric currents and the magnetic fields associated with them carry kinetic energy, like the moving parts in a mechanical system. Electric fields hold potential energy, like mechanical springs. Faraday's electrotonic state is a form of momentum. Electromotive and magnetomotive forces are not forces in the mechanical sense but behave somewhat similarly. For example, an electromotive force acts on an insulating material (or empty space) like a mechanical force acts on a spring, putting it under stress and storing energy. When it tries to do this to a conductor the material gives way, so the force does not build up stress but instead drives a current. With these and similar insights, James tried applying Lagrange's method.

In some ways electromagnetic systems were nothing like mechanical ones; for example, linear electrical forces tended to produce circular magnetic effects and vice versa. James hoped to show that such behaviour followed naturally from the normal laws of dynamics when they were applied to an electromagnetic field. He represented the properties of the whole field mathematically as a set of inter-related quantities which could vary in time and space. To solve the problem he needed to find the mathematical relationship between the quantities at a single arbitrary point, which could be in any kind of material or in empty space. The resulting equations would need to describe how the various quantities interacted with one another in the space immediately surrounding the point, and with time.

Most of these quantities were *vectors*, having a direction as well as a numerical value. The five main vectors were the electric and magnetic field intensities, which resembled forces, the electric and magnetic flux densities, which resembled strains, and the electric current density, which was a kind of flow. One important quantity, electric charge density, was a *scalar*, having only a numerical value. These six quantities were like the ropes and bells connected by the invisible machinery inside the belfry. If one could find the equations connecting them one would know everything about how electromagnetic systems behaved.

One would be able to ring a tune on the bells without knowing anything about the machinery inside.

Everything came together beautifully. James showed that all aspects of the behaviour of electromagnetic systems, including the propagation of light, could, in his interpretation, be derived from the laws of dynamics. Disinclined as he was to crow about his achievements, he could not entirely contain his elation. Towards the end of a long letter to his cousin Charles Hope Cay he wrote:

> I also have a paper afloat, with an electromagnetic theory of light, which, till I am convinced to the contrary, I hold to be great guns.

Great guns indeed. The essence of the theory is embodied in four equations which connect the six main quantities. They are now known to every physicist and electrical engineer as Maxwell's equations. They are majestic mathematical statements, deep and subtle yet startlingly simple. So eloquent are they that one can get a sense of their beauty and power even without advanced mathematical training.

When the equations are applied to a point in empty space, the terms which represent the effects of electric charges and conduction currents are not needed[6]. The equations then become even simpler and take on a wonderful, stark symmetry; here they are[7]:

$$\text{div } \mathbf{E} = 0 \qquad (1)$$

$$\text{div } \mathbf{H} = 0 \qquad (2)$$

$$\text{curl } \mathbf{E} = -(1/c)\ \partial \mathbf{H}/\partial \text{t} \qquad (3)$$

$$\text{curl } \mathbf{H} = (1/c)\ \partial \mathbf{E}/\partial \text{t} \qquad (4)$$

E is the electric force and **H** the magnetic force at our arbitrary point[8]. The bold lettering shows that they are vectors, having both strength and direction. $\partial \mathbf{E}/\partial t$ and $\partial \mathbf{H}/\partial t$, also vectors, are the rates of change of **E** and **H** with time. The constant c acts as a kind of gear ratio between electric and magnetic forces—it is the ratio of the electromagnetic and electrostatic units of charge.

Leaving aside mathematical niceties, the equations can readily be interpreted in everyday terms. The terms 'div' (short for divergence) and 'curl' are ways of representing how the forces **E** and **H** vary in the space immediately surrounding the point. Div is a measure of the tendency of the force to be directed more outwards than inwards (div greater than zero), or more inwards than outwards (div less than zero). Curl, on the other hand, measures the tendency of the force to curl, or loop, around the point and gives the direction of the axis about which it curls.

- Equation (1) says that the electric force in a small region around our point has, on average, no inward or outward tendency. This implies that no electric charge is present.
- Equation (2) says the same for the magnetic force, implying that no single magnetic poles are present: they always come in north/south pairs in any case.
- The first two equations also imply the familiar laws for static fields: that the forces between electric charges and between magnetic poles vary inversely with the square of the distance separating them.
- Equation (3) says that when the magnetic force changes it wraps a circular electric force around itself. The minus sign means that the sense of the electric force is anticlockwise when viewed in the direction of the rate of change of the magnetic force.
- Equation (4) says that when the electric force changes it wraps a circular magnetic force around itself. The sense of the magnetic force is clockwise when viewed in the direction of the rate of change of the electric force.
- In equations (3) and (4) the constant c links the space variation (curl) of the magnetic force to the time variation ($\partial/\partial t$) of the electric force, and vice versa. It has the dimensions of a velocity

and, as Maxwell rightly concluded, is the speed at which electromagnetic waves, including light, travel.

Equations (3) and (4) work together to give us these waves. We can get an idea of what happens simply by looking at the equations. A changing electric force wraps itself with a magnetic force; as that changes it wraps itself in a further layer of electric force and so on. Thus the changes in the combined field of electrical and magnetic forces spread out in a kind of continuous leapfrogging action.

In mathematical terms, equations (3) and (4) are two simultaneous differential equations with two unknowns. It is a simple matter to eliminate **E** and **H** in turn, giving one equation containing only **H** and another containing only **E**. In each case the solution turns out to be a form of equation known to represent a transverse wave travelling with speed c. The **E** and **H** waves always travel together: neither can exist alone. They vibrate at right angles to each other and are always in phase.

Thus any change in either the electrical or magnetic fields sends a combined transverse electromagnetic wave through space at a speed equal to the ratio of the electromagnetic and electrostatic units of charge. As we have seen, this ratio had been experimentally measured and, when put in the right units, was close to experimental measurements of the speed of light. James' electromagnetic theory of light now no longer rested on a speculative model but was founded on the well-established principles of dynamics.

His system of equations worked with jewelled precision. Its construction had been an immense feat of sustained creative effort in three stages spread over 9 years. The whole route was paved with inspired innovations but from a historical perspective one crucial step stands out—the idea that electric currents exist in empty space. It is these *displacement currents* that give the equations their symmetry and make the waves possible. Without them the term $\partial \mathbf{E}/\partial t$ in equation (4) becomes zero and the whole edifice crumbles.

Some accounts of the theory's origin make no mention of the spinning cell model, or dismiss it as a makeshift contrivance which became irrelevant as soon as the dynamical theory appeared. In doing so they wrongly present Maxwell as a coldly cerebral mathematical genius. One can hardly dispute the epithet 'genius', but his thoughts were firmly rooted in the everyday physical world that all of us experience. The keystone of his beautiful theory, the displacement current, had its origin in the idea that the spinning cells in his construction-kit model could be springy.

James published *A Dynamical Theory of the Electromagnetic Field* in seven parts and introduced it at a presentation to the Royal Society in December 1864[9]. Most of his contemporaries were bemused. It was almost as if Einstein had popped out of a time machine to tell them about general relativity; they simply did not know what to make of it. Some thought that abandoning the mechanical model was a backward step; among these was William Thomson, who, for all his brilliance, never came close to understanding Maxwell's theory.

One can understand these reactions. Not only was the theory ahead of its time but James was no evangelist and hedged his presentation with philosophical caution. He thought that his theory was probably right but could not be sure. No-one could until Heinrich Hertz produced and detected electromagnetic waves over 20 years later. The 'great guns' had been paraded but it would be a long while before they sounded.

It is almost impossible to overstate the importance of James' achievement. The fact that its significance was but dimly recognised at the time makes it all the more remarkable. The theory encapsulated some of the most fundamental characteristics of the universe. Not only did it explain all known electromagnetic phenomena, it explained light and pointed to the existence of kinds of radiation not then dreamt of. Professor R. V. Jones was doing no more than representing the common opinion of later scientists when he described the theory as one of the greatest leaps ever achieved in human thought.

The authorities in King's College had no more idea than anyone else of the immense significance of James' electromagnetic theory. But they recognised the importance of his other research and experimental work and appreciated the kudos it brought to the university. They appointed a lecturer to help him with College duties. The first post-holder, George Smalley, left after a year for Australia and eventually became Astronomer Royal at Sydney. His successor was W. Grylls Adams, younger brother of John Couch Adams, in whose honour the Adams' Prize had been founded. Even with this help James was finding it harder each year to fit in all the things he wanted to do. He and Katherine had by now a mass of data on colour vision which needed to be properly analysed and reported. There were ideas he wanted to pursue to extend his theory on gases. He saw a need for a substantial book on electricity and magnetism which would bring order to the subject and help newcomers. And he wanted more time at home, to make further improvements to the house and estate, and to play a more regular role as a leading person in local affairs. He decided to resign his chair so that he and Katherine could take up a settled life at Glenlair.

James handed over the professorship to Adams but agreed to help by returning to give evening lectures to the artisans during the following winter. They had been five good years in London. He had thrived on the variety: College lectures, home experiments on colour vision and gases, the experimental work on electrical standards for the British Association, and his two great papers on electromagnetism. It was wonderful to be able to walk to meetings at the Royal Society and Royal Institution, where he could enjoy the ready companionship of fellow scientists. But he was still a country boy at heart and he and Katherine loved their home. In the spring of 1865 they left their Kensington House for Glenlair.

CHAPTER NINE

THE LAIRD AT HOME

Glenlair 1865–1871

A few weeks before starting at King's College, James had nearly died from smallpox. Soon after leaving there he narrowly survived another misfortune. In the summer of 1865 he scraped his head on the branch of a tree while riding a strange horse and became seriously ill when an infection took hold. For the second time, Katherine's nursing helped him to pull through. He was laid up for a month but recovered fast once the infection had cleared and it was not long before they were riding again.

Over the years James had steadily improved the estate. One splendid new feature was a stone bridge over the Urr where there had been a ford and stepping stones. The bridge, which still stands, was built by his cousin William Dyce Cay, a newly qualified civil engineer. Typical of the encouragement James gave to his young cousins, and to young people generally, was that he had taken the trouble to visit Belfast to arrange for William to study there under the eminent James Thomson, brother of William Thomson. William the cousin went on to become an expert in harbour construction.

The house at Glenlair was modest. It looked like two cottages pushed together, one behind the other. It had been a cherished wish of John Clerk Maxwell to extend it by adding a taller and grander section at one end but the funds did not match the ambition, and he died before the plans could be turned to sandstone and mortar. James had spent many hours helping to draft these plans and knew what pleasure his father drew from anticipating their fulfilment. Now he had a chance to carry out the scheme, albeit on a more economical scale. He went over all the details, made changes where needed, and arranged with builders for the work to be done in the spring and summer of 1867.

The nearest village was Corsock, 3 miles to the north. A church had been built there in 1838 but no provision had been made to pay the minister a proper salary, or to provide a house for him. Most of the people were poor and James had been busy fund-raising among the local gentry and sympathetic friends elsewhere to get the church properly endowed and a manse built. He also contributed generously himself and by 1863 the aim was finally accomplished. By then the church had a fine minister, George Sturrock, who stayed in post for many years and became a prominent figure in the neighbourhood. James had a hand in this happy outcome. When the post became vacant in 1861 he insisted that the newcomer be given a 3 month trial. The person appointed did, indeed, leave after 3 months and the job then came to Sturrock. To mark the church's new status, Corsock was made a Parish, and Glenlair fell within its bounds. James became the first trustee of the parish and an elder of the church.

Something else he took a spirited interest in was local schooling. A later incident may be mentioned here to give an idea of how strongly he felt. The district School Board wanted to close the village school at nearby Merkland. James defended the school and offered to support it at his own expense. When this offer was refused he marked out a site on the Glenlair estate and drew up plans for a new school to be built there. Sadly, the scheme was lost with his early death.

He enjoyed local community life and got on well with neighbours and, especially, their children. Remembering the pleasures of his own childhood, he loved to amuse them with tricks and games. It was clear by now that he and Katherine would have no children of their own: they had been married 8 years; she was 42 and he 35. We do not know why they remained childless but can be sure it was not from choice. Lewis Campbell's affectionate biography makes no mention of the matter and we have no clue from any of James' or Katherine's surviving letters.

Whatever the cause, the lack of children must have cast a shadow over their lives. Not only would they miss the experience of parenthood but also the line of inheritance would be broken. James' father and mother had turned the Glenlair estate from a stony waste to pleasant and productive farmland. He had spent an idyllic childhood there and loved it as well as any man can love his home. Now Glenlair would pass to a cousin to whom it would be simply a country estate. But it was a motto with James that there is no use in thinking of what might have been. Outwardly at least, he put the disappointment to one side.

Although by no means flamboyant or extrovert, James was certainly a man who left an impression on those he met. This is how he appeared to a contemporary who first saw him in 1866:

> A man of middle height, with frame strongly knit, and a certain spring and elasticity in his gait; dressed for comfortable ease rather than elegance; a face expressive at once of sagacity and good humour, but overlaid with a deep shade of thoughtfulness; features boldly but pleasingly marked; eyes dark and glowing; hair and beard perfectly black, and forming a strong contrast to the pallor of his complexion ... He might have been taken, by a careless observer, for a country gentleman, or rather, to be more accurate, for a north country laird. A keener eye would have seen, however, that the man must be a student of some sort, and one of more than ordinary intelligence.

The same correspondent reports his impressions on further acquaintance:

> He had a strong sense of humour, and a keen relish for witty or jocose repartee, but rarely betrayed enjoyment

> by outright laughter. The outward sign and conspicuous manifestation of his enjoyment was a peculiar twinkle and brightness of the eyes. There was, indeed, nothing explosive in his mental composition, and as his mirth was never boisterous, so neither was he fretful or irascible. Of a serenely placid temper, genial and temperate in his enjoyments, and infinitely patient when others would have been vexed or annoyed, he at all times opposed a solid calm of nature to the vicissitudes of life.[1]

James had always been a prolific letter writer. Now that Glenlair was his professional as well as his private address, consignments of journals, manuscripts and proofs started to come in, adding to a growing daily bundle of personal and business letters. To ease the postman's burden, James had a post box set into the rough stone wall by the side of the road, about half a mile from the house. It was a good system. Every day he walked down the drive to take outgoing letters and parcels to the postbox and pick up the incoming mail, at the same time giving the dogs a run.

Among the correspondents were his old school friend P. G. Tait, who had beaten him to the professorship of natural philosophy at Edinburgh University, and William Thomson, who had long held the corresponding post at Glasgow University and was now getting rich from patents and consultancy work on the Atlantic telegraph. The three great Scottish physicists had for years written to each other sharing ideas, comments and gossip. Now this burgeoned into an exuberant, quick-fire three-way exchange. They often used postcards, for speed and convenience, and developed a jokey kind of code language so as to get as much as possible on a card. James and Tait had done this sort of thing as schoolboys and drew just as much delight from it now as then. Thomson probably looked on it all with benign tolerance, but he played along.

Names were the first things to be abbreviated: Thomson was T, Tait was T′. James became dp/dt, from an equation in Tait's book on thermodynamics, dp/dt = JCM. Hermann Helmholtz, whom they admired, was H^2. John Tyndall, who was not held in such high regard, was T''. Tait, whose benevolence to all men was rather less than James', said privately that this was because Tyndall was a second order quantity. Alexander Macmillan, the publisher, was #, because he was a sharp character. Greek letters were useful in quasi-phonetic abbreviations: $\Sigma\phi\alpha\rho\xi$ stood for spherical harmonics and $\theta\Delta$ics for thermodynamics.

Their feeling of common regard was so secure that it could withstand the most robust ribbing. Here, in a report to the Royal Society of Edinburgh, James pokes fun at Tait's increasing fondness for brevity in his mathematical writing, which made some of the steps hard to follow:

> I beg leave to report that I consider the first two pages of Professor Tait's Paper on Orthogonal Isothermal Surfaces as deserving and requiring to be printed in the Transactions of the R.S.E. as a rare and valuable example of the manner of that Master in his middle or Transition period, previous to that remarkable condensation of his style, which has rendered it impenetrable to all but the piercing intellect of the author in his best moments.

Thomson and Tait were collaborating on their *Treatise on Natural Philosophy*, which attempted to map out the state of all aspects of physics, a huge undertaking. They asked James to check drafts of some of the chapters and got exactly the sort of constructive criticism a good author welcomes: as we have seen, he picked them up on the definition of mass. James was himself starting to compile his *Treatise on Electricity and Magnetism*, encompassing with rigour everything that was known on the topic. This was a monumental task, which was to take him 7 years.

The 6 years James spent at Glenlair were not in any sense a time of retirement. On the contrary, this was, by any standards, an outstandingly prolific period. Apart from preparing the *Treatise*, he published a book, *The Theory of Heat*, and 16 papers on an amazingly diverse range of topics, all with something profoundly original to say. We shall come to these later in the chapter.

He and Katherine did, however, find time for a touring holiday in Italy in the spring and early summer of 1867 while the house was being extended. It was usual in those days for anyone with enough money and leisure to make 'the grand tour' of the cultural and historical high spots. The Maxwells' life style was far removed from that of the fashionable set and the holiday was one of their few extravagances. The first adventure was not one they had sought; their ship was put under quarantine at Marseilles. James' fortitude came to the fore. Harking back to his childhood at Glenlair, he became the general water-carrier, and in other ways did everything possible to ease the discomfort of fellow passengers.

In Florence they happened by chance to bump into Lewis Campbell and his wife. Campbell later recalled how his friend's enthusiasm for Italian architecture and music brought to mind reports he had read of 'the joy of Michelangelo in etherealising the work of Brunelleschi'. Not that James was ever reverential; in his account the Vatican orchestra became 'the Pope's band'. He and Katherine took lessons in Italian and he quickly became fluent enough to discuss scientific matters with an Italian colleague in Pisa. He also took every chance of improving his French and German by talking to fellow tourists, but found himself at a loss with Dutch.

There were other breaks from home. Each spring James and Katherine stayed in London for several weeks and James travelled to British Association meetings in various parts of the country, sometimes acting as president of the Mathematics and Physics Section. He also made annual visits to Cambridge. The University had asked him to act as moderator, then examiner, for the Mathematical Tripos. This was an inspired move, possibly prompted by William Thomson, who had been appointed a public examiner. Cambridge had pulled itself out of a mathematical rut in the early 1800s, thanks to the efforts of Charles Babbage and some of his colleagues, but was now settling into a broader scientific one. The Mathematical Tripos exam was partly to blame. Its questions were still like those in James' student days. A contemporary described them as 'mathematical trifles and problems, so called, barren alike of practical results and scientific interest'. James set about making the examinations more interesting and more relevant to everyday experience, as he had done at King's College. It was the start of a magnificent revival of Cambridge's scientific tradition, in which James was yet to play the main part.

Ever since his brilliant but flawed paper of 1860 on gas theory, James had been mulling over new ideas on the topic. In 1866 he brought them to fruition in a paper, *On the Dynamical Theory of Gases*. His earlier paper had given the world its first statistical law of physics—the Maxwell distribution of molecular velocities—and had predicted that the viscosity of a gas was independent of its pressure, a remarkable result which James and Katherine had verified by experiment in their Kensington attic. In other parts of the paper he had made errors in calculation, which were embarrassing but easily corrected.

His results had greatly advanced and strengthened the theory that gases consist of myriads of jostling molecules, but two serious problems remained. One was to do with the ratio of the specific heat of air at constant pressure to that at constant volume; the theory predicted a different value from that observed in practice. As we shall see, the answer to this was to prove beyond the reach of nineteenth century scientists. The other problem was more amenable: James' and Katherine's own experiments had shown that the viscosity of a gas did *not* vary with the square root of its absolute temperature, although the theory predicted that it should. The fault seemed to lie in James' original assumption that when molecules collided they behaved like billiard balls, in other words that they were perfectly elastic spheres. He now tried the alternative assumption that they did not actually come into contact at all but repelled one another with a force that varied inversely with the *n*th power of the separation distance: if *n* was, say, 4 or larger, the repulsive force would be great when two molecules came close together but negligible when they were far apart. Some fiendishly complicated mathematics followed because the molecules no longer travelled in straight lines but followed complex curves.

He found two ways to simplify the calculations. One was to introduce the notion of *relaxation time*, the time a system takes to return to a state of equilibrium after being disturbed. This is a concept now routinely used throughout physics and engineering. One can, for example, easily picture its application to car suspension systems. Like so many of Maxwell's innovations, it has become so familiar that one wonders why nobody had thought of it before.

The other simplification arose, amazingly, when repulsion between molecules varied inversely as the 5th power of separation distance. When he put $n = 5$ in his equations, all the terms concerning the relative velocities of molecules cancelled out, leaving much simpler relationships. And there was a bonus: viscosity now became directly proportional to absolute temperature, in line with his own experimental results in the Kensington attic. This particular triumph was short-lived, as more accurate experiments by others showed that the relationship was not linear after all. But a later generation of experimenters found that some kinds of molecules do indeed seem to follow an inverse 5th power repulsion law. For those that do not, physicists still find Maxwell's formulae useful as a starting point for more exact calculations.

Even with the simplifications, the mathematical obstacles were as formidable as those James had faced when tackling Saturn's rings. He overcame them with such mastery that some scholars consider this the most inspiring of all his works. The young Ludwig Boltzmann, already working on his own first great paper, was entranced. The mastery was not easily achieved. At one stage James almost threw in the towel when some of his equations predicted perpetual motion currents in the earth's atmosphere. He found his mistake, then had to search for and correct a further mistake in the revised calculations. Doggedness won the day. James was able to work out formulae not only for viscosity but for diffusion, heat conduction and other properties, which agreed with known experimental results. It was a seminal paper. He had not only corrected and extended his earlier work but had greatly strengthened the theory that gases (and, by extension, all forms of matter) were composed of molecules. Most of all, he had set the theory on a firm base, on which he, Boltzmann and others could build.

The work of the British Association's committee on electrical standards had not stopped with the production of a standard of resistance. The next task on their agenda stemmed from James' prediction of electromagnetic waves which travelled at a speed equal to the ratio of the electromagnetic and electrostatic units of charge. As we have seen, an earlier measurement of this ratio by Kohlrausch and Weber, once converted to the appropriate units, was very close to Fizeau's measurement of the speed of light, thus supporting James' theory that light itself was composed of electromagnetic waves. This result was so important that the evidence needed to be checked; a new experiment was urgently needed to corroborate Kohlrausch and Weber's result. It would be a difficult experiment and at best the range of possible error would be a few percent, but it had to be done.

This time James' chief collaborator was Charles Hockin, of St John's College, Cambridge. They decided to try to balance the electrostatic attraction between two charged metal plates against the magnetic repulsion between two current-carrying coils, and built a balance arm apparatus to do this. For this method to work they needed a very high voltage source. The biggest batteries in Britain were owned by a Clapham wine merchant, John Peter Gassiot, who had acquired them for his private laboratory. Gassiot was delighted to act as host for the experiment and furnished his guests with a battery of 2600 cells, giving about 3000 volts.

James arranged to do the experiment during his 1868 spring visit to London. It was not easy work. First they had to take precautions to stop electricity leaking from the great battery through the laboratory floor. Then they had to become expert at taking readings at speed because the batteries ran down so quickly. When these problems had been overcome, the experiment gave a value for the ratio of the two units of charge, and hence for the speed of James' waves, of 288,000 kilometres per second.

This was about 7% below the value which Kohlrausch and Weber had obtained for the electromagnetic/electrostatic units ratio and 8% below the speed of light as measured by Fizeau (the two results James had quoted in his paper). And it was 3% below a new measurement of the speed of light by Fizeau's compatriot Foucault. James must have felt a tinge of disappointment that the correspondence was not closer but in logical terms the experiment was a success. His theory that light consisted of electromagnetic waves now stood on stronger ground because two independent experimental results gave predicted wave speeds which, given reasonable allowance for experimental error, corresponded to the measured speed of the light. We now know that the true speed of light is about mid-way between that predicted by James' experiment and that predicted by Weber's[2].

James produced a dazzling array of publications on other topics during his Glenlair period. A few examples will give an idea of their astonishing scope and originality.

The nineteenth century was the age of the steam engine and great strides had been made in the understanding of heat, through the work of Carnot, Clausius, Joule, Thomson, Rankine and others. James wrote what was originally intended as nothing more than an elementary introduction to the subject: *The Theory of Heat*. It was indeed a good introduction to the established theory but also included a completely new formulation of the relationships between the main quantities: pressure, volume, temperature and entropy*. By a geometrical argument, he

* Entropy is a measure of the disorder in a system. According to the second law of thermodynamics, it always tends to increase. A small change of entropy is defined as the amount of heat transferred in a reversible process divided by the temperature at which the heat is transferred.

expressed these relationships as differential equations in a form which turned out to be extremely useful. They are now part of the standard repertoire and are known as Maxwell relations.

The Theory of Heat also introduced readers to James' most extraordinary invention: an imaginary, molecule-sized being who could make heat flow from a cold substance to a hot one, thereby defying the second law of thermodynamics. This was *Maxwell's demon*[3]. The little creature soon took on legendary status and lived up to its name, perplexing the world's best physicists for 60 years. William Thomson gets the credit for the name.

Playful though it was, James' idea was also a profound 'thought experiment' of the kind that Einstein later made his own. The demon guards a small hole in the wall separating two compartments of a container filled with gas. He has a shutter over the hole which he can open when he wants to. Molecules in both compartments are moving in all directions. Their average speed (strictly, the average of the square of their speeds) determines the temperature of the gas (the faster the hotter) and, to start with, this is the same on both sides of the wall.

According to James' own law for the distribution of velocities, some molecules are moving slower than the average speed and some faster. When the demon sees a fast molecule in the right compartment approaching the hole he opens the shutter briefly and lets it through to the left side. Similarly, he lets slow molecules pass from the left compartment to the right. The rest of the time he keeps the shutter closed.

With each exchange the average speed of molecules in the left compartment increases and that in the right compartment falls. But there will still be some molecules in the right compartment travelling faster than the average speed in the left and when one of these approaches the shutter the demon lets it through. In the same way, he continues to let slow molecules through from left to right. So the gas in the left compartment gets steadily hotter while that in the right compartment gets colder.

The demon is making heat flow from a colder gas on the right to the hotter gas on the left, thus defying the second law of thermodynamics, which says that heat cannot flow from a colder to a hotter body. By the same token, the demon is providing the means of making a perpetual motion machine: the temperature difference between the gases could be harnessed to make a machine do physical work; the machine would keep going until the temperature difference fell back to zero; we would then be back where we started and could repeat the process until all the heat energy in the gas had been converted into work[4].

Of course, this cannot really happen. The interesting question is why not? James' gave two explanations. The first was that the second law of thermodynamics is, at root, a *statistical* law. As he put it, the law is equivalent to the statement that if you throw a tumblerful of water into the sea, you cannot get the same tumblerful out again; it applies to molecules *en masse*, not to individuals. This was indeed correct, but his other explanation, although apparently light-hearted, turned out to be even more penetrating. He said that if we were sufficiently nimble fingered, like the demon, we could break the second law 'only we can't, not being clever enough'.

Why aren't we as clever as the demon? To match him we would have to know the positions and velocities of all the molecules. Leo Szilard, in 1929, showed that the very act of acquiring information about a system increases its entropy in proportion to the amount of information gathered. As the entropy increases, less of the system's total heat energy is available for doing work. To gather enough information to work the shutter effectively we would have to use up, or render inaccessible, an amount of energy at least equal to the work output of any machine that we could drive from the system. So we will never be clever enough to create perpetual motion.

Through the work of Szilard and others, Maxwell's demon helped to spark the creation of information theory, now an essential part of the theoretical basis of communications and computing.

In the experiment at King's to establish a standard for electrical resistance, James had used a governor to keep the coil spinning at a constant rate. This had turned his thoughts to the way governors worked. In a steam engine governor, weights on a driven shaft are linked to a valve controlling the steam input. The further the weights fly out under centrifugal force, the smaller the valve opening becomes. If the engine starts to speed up the steam input is reduced, causing it to slow again; so the engine settles down to a controlled steady speed. James saw that the same principle could be applied to give precise and stable control of any kind of machine.

The key idea was negative feedback. To control the machine's output to a desired value (which may vary over time), you continuously compare the actual output against the required output, and feed the difference back to the input in such a way as to make the output converge on the wanted value. James worked out the conditions for stability under various feedback arrangements, and examined the effects of damping and of changes in the driven load. He wrote up the results in a paper called *On Governors*. It was the first mathematical analysis of control systems and became the foundation of modern control theory.

Amazingly, the work attracted little attention until the 1940s, when control systems were urgently needed for military equipment during the second world war. Engineers were then pleased to find that Maxwell had already worked out the basis of the theory they needed. After the war Norbert Wiener took things further and developed the science of cybernetics.

James had a knack of finding ways in which the natural world followed mathematical principles. A delightful example was his paper *On Hills and Dales*. The earth's surface has high areas or hills, each with a summit, and low areas, each with a bottom point, which James called an 'immit'. There are also ridges, valleys or dales, and passes. He saw that the numbers of each of these features must be somehow related by mathematical rules and set about working them out. One of the simpler rules he found is that the number of summits is always one more than the number of passes. The branch of mathematics dealing with the spatial relationships of things, irrespective of their sizes or shapes, was then called the geometry of position. It was in its infancy and James was breaking new ground, helping to pave the way for what has become the deep and complex subject of topology. His results in *On Hills and Dales* are also relevant to meteorology; the formulae apply equally well to an air pressure system with its highs, lows, troughs and ridges. Moreover, James' original ideas about the earth's surface have themselves now developed into a serious branch of topology called global analysis.

James expanded the ideas which began in the paper he had written at King's College on how to calculate forces in frameworks by using reciprocal diagrams, eventually extending the method to continuous media. The Royal Society of Edinburgh acclaimed this work by awarding him its Keith Medal. He also developed the underlying principle of duality, on which reciprocal diagrams depend, and went on to show how it could be applied to such diverse topics as electrical circuits and optics.

James wrote most of his *Treatise on Electricity and Magnetism* during the period at Glenlair but, as it was not published until 1873, we will leave its description until our next chapter. On the way to the *Treatise* he published a fairly short paper, *Note on the Electromagnetic Theory of Light*. Here he gave a more compact derivation and formulation of the main equations from his *Dynamical Theory* and produced arguments to show that rival theories from Wilhelm Weber and Bernhard Riemann, which both postulated action at a distance rather than through an energy-carrying field, could not be true because they defied the laws of conservation of energy. As always, he couldn't resist poking a little fun:

> From the assumptions of both these papers we may draw the conclusions, first, that action and reaction are not equal and opposite, and second, that apparatus may be constructed to generate any amount of work from its resources.

Being essentially three-dimensional, the electromagnetic field posed a problem in mathematical notation. In his papers, James had so far written each relation involving vectors as a triple set of equations: one part for each of the x, y and z directions. This was cumbersome and made it hard to see the wood for the trees. But at least it was a notation people understood: it was difficult enough for them to cope with a new kind of theory; to have expected them to learn a new notation at the same time would have been unreasonable.

Nowadays we use the compact notation of vector analysis, in which each triple (x, y, z) set of equations is replaced by a single vector equation, where a single symbol embodies the x, y and z components of a vector quantity like force or velocity. Its precursor was the system of 'quaternions' invented by the great Irish mathematician Sir William Rowan Hamilton (not to be confused with Sir William Hamilton who had taught James philosophy at Edinburgh University). Quaternions are more complicated than vectors because they each have *four* components: a scalar part, which is just a number, and a vector part with components in each of the x, y and z directions. Our modern vector system dispenses with the scalar part.

Quaternions were not easy to get to grips with and only a few enthusiasts wanted anything to do with them. The foremost of these was James' friend P. G. Tait. But they had the advantage of great compactness. In some of James' equations nine ordinary symbols could by replaced by two quaternion terms. James found that they also made the physical meaning of the equations clearer. He decided to include the shorthand quaternion representation in his *Treatise*, alongside the conventional longhand notation: ploughing with an ox and an ass together, as he put it.

To help with the physical interpretation of his equations, James coined the terms '*curl*', '*convergence*' and '*gradient*' for use in quaternion representation. Curl and convergence represent two kinds of space variation of vectors and are the terms used today, except that convergence is replaced by its negative, '*divergence*', or *div* for short. Gradient, abbreviated to *grad*, is also used today; it represents the direction and rate of change of a scalar quantity in space. James had started the process that was to give us the elegant and relatively simple system of modern vector analysis, which is now so widely used that we take it for granted. The job was completed around 20 years later by two outstanding physicists, the American Josiah Willard Gibbs and the Englishman Oliver Heaviside.

James set up his colour box again and more guests were invited to have a go at matching colours. He summarised his accumulated results in two short papers, one of which dealt with colour vision at different points in the retina. Here James reported his investigation of the 'yellow spot', a small yellow region near the centre of the retina. He had found that most, but not all, people have much reduced colour perception in that region. The exceptional people had a yellow spot that was so faintly yellow as to be imperceptible. He also found a way to detect whether a person has a perceptible yellow spot without examining the retina; this is now called the Maxwell spot test. Katherine was among those with no discernable yellow spot but by now it was clear that she was in a very small minority. As James explained to a friend:

> I can exhibit the yellow spot to all who have it—and all have it except Col. Strange, F.R.S., my late father in law, and my wife—whether they be Negroes, Jews, Parsees, Armenians, Russians, Italians, Germans, Frenchmen, Poles, etc. Professor Pole, for instance, has it nearly as strong as me, though he is colour-blind; Mathison, also colour blind, being fair, has it less strongly marked.[5]

Among the Maxwells' most frequent guests at Glenlair were his young Cay cousins: William, who had built the new bridge over the Urr, and Charles, who had embarked on a teaching career and was now mathematics master at Clifton College, near Bristol. Charles, especially, was like a young brother to James and a great favourite with both of them. Katherine named her pony, Charlie, after him, and it was with Charles that James had shared the elation he felt about his 'great guns' paper on electromagnetism. Things were going well for Charles; he was popular at the school and had been made a housemaster. But in 1869 there came the tragic news that he had died, bringing a great sense of loss to the Maxwell household.

And there was sadness from another quarter; James' old mentor and friend James Forbes died at about the same time. When Forbes had left his chair of natural philosophy at Edinburgh in 1860 to become Principal of St Andrews University, James had applied for the Edinburgh post but been turned down in favour of his friend Tait. Now James was asked by several of the professors at St Andrews to consider standing for the principalship. They included Lewis Campbell, who was now Professor of Greek there. At first James was reluctant. He had left King's because he wanted to live at Glenlair and the attractions of home life were just as great now. And he was not sure that he was cut out for the job, feeling that: 'my proper line is in working not in governing, still less in reigning and letting others govern'. But he did believe passionately in good education; maybe he could do some good in the post. And his supporters were very enthusiastic.

He was persuaded first to visit St Andrews, a long day's travel each way in those days, and then to let his name go forward. This was a politically sensitive appointment and much would hinge on the political influence of the referees put forward by candidates. James was a political novice. William Thomson's public standing was great enough to transcend politics, but who else should he ask for letters of recommendation? He wrote to a London acquaintance:

> I have paid so little attention to the political sympathies of scientific men that I do not know which of the scientific men I am acquainted with have the ear of the Government. If you can inform me, it would be of service to me.[6]

Given such candid naivety, it is perhaps not surprising that James did not get the post. It went to J. C. Shairp, professor of Latin at the University. Whatever his other merits, Shairp had two clear points in his favour. He was a supporter of Gladstone's Liberal party, which came into power shortly before the appointment was made, and a friend of the Duke of Argyll, who was Chancellor of the University.

A surprising footnote to this episode is that St Andrews had also turned down James Prescott Joule, the outstanding experimental physicist who had established the equivalence of work and heat, for their professorship of natural philosophy. It seems that Joule had a slight personal deformity which disqualified him in the view of one of the electors[7].

Except for his first appointment at Aberdeen, James' experiences with Scottish Universities were, to say the least, discouraging: he was made redundant by Aberdeen, then rejected in turn by Edinburgh and St Andrews. But life at Glenlair was good and in any event his 'proper line' was 'in working not in governing'.

After his Edinburgh rejection, he had been welcomed by King's College, London. Now the sequence was repeated. In February 1871 he was asked by Cambridge University to accept an important new professorship in experimental physics. The Duke of Devonshire, who was Chancellor of the University, had offered a large sum of money for the building of a new laboratory for teaching and research, and the first professor would have the dual task of starting up the department and getting the laboratory built. Cambridge was being left behind in experimental science by several British universities and many continental ones. This was a great opportunity for Cambridge to move up with the leaders. To make the most of it they had to recruit an outstanding professor.

Ideally, they wanted a top scientist who already had experience in running a thriving teaching and research laboratory. The obvious choice was William Thomson. He was approached but did not want to leave Glasgow University, where he had over the years built up a superb research centre, starting in a converted wine cellar. Hermann Helmholtz was also sounded out but he was about to take up a prestigious job in Berlin and declined. James was third choice. The authorities at Cambridge probably regarded him as brilliant, but something of a maverick with his strange theory of electromagnetism. And although he had given demonstration experiments to students and done private research he had no direct experience of *running* a research laboratory.

Still, he was a popular choice among the younger fellows. J. W. Strutt, afterwards Lord Rayleigh and Maxwell's successor in the post, spoke for many in imploring him to come.

As he had been when the St Andrews post was mooted, James was at first reluctant. At length he was persuaded, although only on the understanding that he might retire after a year if he wished. This condition did not imply any lack of commitment. He saw what a great opportunity the scheme offered for Cambridge and the country and felt the excitement, but was acutely conscious of his lack of experience in directing a big operation and wanted to be able to withdraw if he found he was not able to run the show well. James was appointed in March 1871 and moved with Katherine to Cambridge.

CHAPTER TEN

THE CAVENDISH

Cambridge 1871–1879

It was straight down to business at Cambridge. The first task was to draw up a detailed specification for the new laboratory building. Any mistakes at this stage would be expensive or impossible to put right later, so James visited the best university laboratories in the country, including William Thomson's in Glasgow, to learn all he could from their experiences. The character of the new building began to take shape. It would need to have tall windows to give good light, clear corridors and stairwells to serve as laboratory spaces for experiments needing exceptional horizontal or vertical distances, a workshop, a battery room, and a 50 foot tower to provide enough water pressure to drive a powerful vacuum pump. The job of producing a design to meet these and a host of other requirements was given to the architect W. M. Fawcett.

The outcome of Maxwell and Fawcett's work was a splendid testament to their skill and sense: a solid, functional building that seemed to exude confidence about its place in the scheme of things. It became the birthplace of much of modern physics and served Cambridge well for 100 years.

The cheapest tender for the building work was about 30% above the sum originally allocated, but the Duke of Devonshire generously agreed to meet the cost and to pay for the apparatus needed to get the laboratory started. James gave his own equipment to the laboratory and bought several hundred pounds' worth of new apparatus from his own pocket during his tenure. After building work began in 1872 progress was reasonable but it must have seemed agonisingly slow to everyone waiting to get experiments started. Some of the delays tried even James' patience, as he told Lewis Campbell:

> At present I am all day at the Laboratory, which is emerging from chaos, but is not yet clear of gas-men, who are the laziest and most permanent of all the gods who have been hatched under heaven.

Despite the frustrations, James was by now thoroughly immersed in the great enterprise and seems to have given no thought to the get-out clause in his contract. Lectures began while the building was under construction and he had to improvise his own accommodation.

> I have no place to erect my chair, but move about like the cuckoo, depositing my notions in the Chemical lecture-room 1st term; in the Botanical in Lent, and in Comparative Anatomy in Easter.

Experimental work began in the spring of 1874. The building had been known as the Devonshire laboratory but at James' suggestion it was now formally named the Cavendish, thereby commemorating not only the Duke but also his great uncle Henry Cavendish, who was one of the most brilliant scientists—and one of the most misanthropic men—who ever lived. The Duke himself was no mere figurehead. In his student days at Cambridge he had, like James, been second wrangler and first Smith's Prizeman, and he had come to the chancellorship after an active political career. His patronage of the new laboratory stemmed from a passionate belief in the value of scientific education and a feeling that Britain was trailing well behind other countries in its pursuit. During the 1870s the Duke headed a Royal Commission which recommended radical reform after finding evidence that amply confirmed his fears. The recommendations were largely ignored.

There was, of course, an inaugural lecture—James' third. This one had a farcical side-show. Through some misunderstanding a group of senior professors came to his first ordinary lecture to undergraduates, believing it to be the formal event. Never one to miss a joke, James solemnly explained to them and the rest of his class the difference between the Centigrade and Fahrenheit temperature scales.

In the real inaugural lecture he developed several themes that were by now firmly embedded in his philosophy. One was that precise experimental techniques were important in research, not just to improve accuracy for its own sake but as a way of finding the routes to great new regions of science:

> This characteristic of modern experiments—that they consist principally of measurements—is so prominent, that the opinion seems to have got abroad that in a few years all the great physical constants will have been approximately estimated, and that the only occupation which will be left to men of science will be to carry on these measurements to another place of decimals.
>
> ... But the history of science shows that even during that phase of her progress in which she devotes herself to improving the accuracy of the numerical measurement of quantities with which she has long been familiar, she is preparing materials for the subjugation of new regions, which would have remained unknown if she had been contented with the rough methods of her early pioneers. I might bring forward instances gathered from every branch of science, shewing how the labour of careful measurement has been rewarded by the discovery of new fields of research, and by the development of new scientific ideas.

A quarter of a century later, the electron was discovered at the Cavendish Laboratory by Maxwell's next-but-one successor, J. J. Thomson.

Another theme was that people learnt in different ways and that he proposed to use all available methods to teach them. He had made this point graphically in a previous talk to the British Association:

> The human mind is seldom satisfied, and is certainly never exercising its highest functions, when it is doing the work of a calculating machine ... There are, as I have said, some minds which can go on contemplating with satisfaction pure quantities represented to the eye by symbols, and to the mind in a form which none but mathematicians can conceive. There are others who feel more enjoyment in following geometrical forms, which they draw on paper, or build up in the empty space before them. Others, again, are not content unless they can project their whole physical energies into the scene which they conjure up. They learn at what a rate the planets rush through space, and they experience a delightful feeling of exhilaration. They calculate the forces with which the heavenly bodies pull at one another, and they feel their own muscles straining with the effort. To such men momentum, energy, mass are not mere abstract expressions of the results of scientific enquiry. They are words of power, which stir their souls like the memories of childhood.
>
> For the sake of persons of these different types, scientific truth should be presented in different forms, and should be regarded as equally scientific, whether it appears in the robust form and the vivid colouring of a physical illustration, or in the tenuity and paleness of a symbolic expression.[1]

In the inaugural lecture he took the argument further:

> ... we may find illustrations of the highest doctrines of science in games and gymnastics, in travelling by land and by water, in storms of the air and of the sea, and wherever there is matter in motion.

He still had the fascination with the whole physical world that he had felt as a child. In his view, the proper study of science required full use of all one's physical senses and mental powers, both analytical and imaginative. And science was universal, not just something that went on in laboratories. All the same, laboratories had a vital role in teaching and research and he wanted the Cavendish to meet the highest standards in both.

Towards the end of the inaugural lecture he emphasised the *cultural* significance of science:

> We admit that the proper study of mankind is man. But is the student of science to be withdrawn from the study of man, or cut off from every noble feeling, so long as he lives in intellectual fellowship with men who have devoted their lives to the discovery of truth, and the results of whose enquiries have impressed themselves on the ordinary speech and way of thinking of men who have never heard their names? Or is the student of history and of man to omit from his consideration the history of the origin and diffusion of those ideas which have produced so great a difference between one age of the world and another?

All new ventures have their detractors, and James had his full share with the Cavendish project. One diminishing but still powerful school of critics held that, while experiments were necessary in research, they brought no benefit to teaching. A typical member was Isaac Todhunter, the celebrated mathematical tutor, who argued that the only evidence a student needed of a scientific truth was the word of his teacher, who was 'probably a clergyman of mature knowledge, recognised ability, and blameless character'. One afternoon James bumped into Todhunter on King's Parade and invited him to pop into the Cavendish to see a demonstration of conical refraction. Horrified, Todhunter replied: 'No, I have been teaching it all my life and don't want my ideas upset by seeing it now!'[2].

Another group of denigrators were the cynics. Even the respected new journal *Nature* was doubtful of the Cavendish's prospects, suggesting that with luck it might in 10 years reach the standard of a provincial German University.

Despite such dismal predictions, James had no difficulty in gathering a set of talented researchers. Some gave up good posts elsewhere to come to work with him. Had James wanted, he could easily have set people to work on problems arising directly from his own investigations. But that was not his way. He had not taken the job to found a Maxwell school but to help physical science advance on a broad front and to help individual students develop their own powers; and he believed that these ends would be best served if everyone was free to follow his own path. There may have been another reason. It was important for the Cavendish to establish its reputation with some early successes, and the kinds of investigation suggested by his own electromagnetic theory were too difficult and risky for this purpose.

James gave beginners problems that were interesting but not too daunting, started them off and kept a fatherly interest in progress. Some of his students were already experienced researchers. For them he would suggest a topic if asked, but if someone had a firm idea of what he wanted to do James simply encouraged him to get on with it. As we have seen, James' talents as a lecturer were limited. But as a supervising coach in a laboratory he was truly inspirational. Advice from one of the greatest scientific minds of all time was dispensed with unfailing generosity and humour. His students loved him.

The resulting programme of research work consisted in the main of high-precision measurements of fundamental physical quantities. This was important, if unspectacular, work. The subject of electricity and magnetism was still in need of experimental consolidation in some basic areas. For one thing, Ohm's law, the basic law of electrical circuits, had never been thoroughly verified by experiment and was now being called into question. What was in doubt was whether the *resistance* of a given wire (the ratio of voltage to current) under fixed conditions would be the same for any value of current. A student from Aberdeen, George Chrystal, took this work on and was immediately faced with a problem: resistance was known to vary with temperature, and the more current a wire carries, the hotter it gets. Undaunted, he found a way to compensate for the temperature effect and carried out tests using a vast range of currents: the smallest was barely measurable and the largest was great enough to make the wire red hot. The work had to be done with immense care and took 5 months but Ohm's law came out triumphant. Over the whole range of currents the resistance of his sample wire changed by less than one part in a million million.

The Cavendish did not drive off its critics overnight. There were inevitably some complaints from people who unreasonably expected instant benefits. But as it steadily began to produce results of solid worth the voices of the doubters faded away and the Laboratory was on its way to becoming a national institution.

Even more impressive than its early research results was the way it developed the talents of its researchers. Many went on to distinguish themselves elsewhere. Among James' students were Richard Glazebrook, who became the founding Director of the National Physical Laboratory; William Napier Shaw, who got meteorology established as a profession in Britain; James Butcher, who became a successful lawyer and a Tory Member of Parliament and was ennobled as Lord Danesfort; Donald MacAlister, who became President of the General Medical Council and Principal of Glasgow University; and a clutch of professors at other universities, among whom Ambrose Fleming invented the thermionic valve and J. H. Poynting the vector that bears his name*.

James' heart cannot have leapt with joy when, in 1874, the Duke passed him a mass of unpublished accounts of electrical experiments done by his great uncle Henry Cavendish between 1771 and 1781, with a suggestion that he consider editing them for publication. He already had his hands full with the Laboratory and other commitments, and wanted time to pursue his own research. But after a scan through the papers he was captivated by the elegance, originality and power of Cavendish's work. Here

*The Poynting vector is much used in telecommunications work; it represents the energy flow per unit area of an electromagnetic wave.

were some of the finest experiments ever performed; they included important discoveries which had since been attributed to others. To James, scientific facts were incomplete without the knowledge of how they came to be discovered. The process of discovery held as much interest as the result. Scientific history was at least as important as political history and needed to be complete. He decided to undertake the huge task of editing the papers himself —'walking the plank' with them, as he put it in a letter to William Thomson.

Most writers about Maxwell regret that he gave so much time in his last few years to this work, rather than to his own research. From our distant viewpoint it does indeed seem a regrettable decision. But James was not to know he had only 5 years to live. His ideas on electromagnetism and gas theory were still developing and could safely be consigned for a while to 'the department of the mind conducted independently of consciousness', to be 'run off clear' later. And perhaps we should in any case judge the decision by his own motto, 'It's no use thinking of the chap you might have been'. He did what he did because he was a man of genuine altruism and generous spirit.

Henry Cavendish, by contrast, was the meanest curmudgeon imaginable. He had lived as a recluse, venturing out only occasionally for scientific meetings and communicating with his domestic staff by written notes. Women servants were sacked if they allowed themselves to come into his sight. An acquaintance said: 'He probably uttered fewer words in the course of his life than any man who ever lived to fourscore years, not at all excepting the monks of La Trappe'[3]. But his scientific work, begun with his father and continued for many years alone, was sublime. Sometimes he published his findings but more often did not. He could never remember what he had published and what he hadn't, and often confused readers by referring to earlier unpublished results. Cavendish's genius was in performing amazingly accurate experiments with the crudest of equipment by dint of brilliant design and single-minded determination. In one famous experiment he had discovered that water was a

compound, not an element. In another he had measured the density of the earth to within 2% of its true value. But he had published almost none of his electrical work and the great bulk of it came to James in the form of manuscripts about 100 years old.

Cavendish's electrical experiments were a revelation. Among a series of outstanding results, he had demonstrated the inverse square law of force between electric charges more effectively than Coulomb, after whom the law was named, and he had discovered Ohm's law 50 years before Ohm. The way he did this in the days before batteries and current meters evokes images from a Gothic novel. He charged up an electrical storage device, connected it to a circuit with two open terminals, discharged it through his body by putting a hand across the terminals and noted how far up his arm he could feel the shock. His staunch servant Richard would then take his place and Cavendish would make a note of his reactions. The procedure was repeated using different circuit arrangements, each time measuring the current by the severity of the shock.

The experiment was not as horrific as it sounds. James repeated it in the Cavendish Laboratory and found that horny-handed rowers had a higher electrical resistance than the other students. One day a distinguished American called in to see James and was surprised to find the great man with sleeves rolled up, preparing to wire himself in. When invited to have a go himself the visitor took fright and left, saying 'When an English man of science comes to the United States we do not treat him like that'[4].

The account of Henry Cavendish's work was fed in sections to the publishers. James went to immense trouble to write an interesting and accurate narrative, even checking such details as whether the Royal Society premises in 1771 had a garden. The book was eventually published in 1879, a few weeks before James' death[5].

Another big commitment James took on was the joint scientific editorship, with T. H. Huxley, of the 9th edition of the *Encyclopaedia*

Britannica. Like his work on the Cavendish papers, this was a labour of love. He believed passionately in the value of good popular presentation of science and wrote many of the encyclopaedia articles himself, as well as others for journals such as *Nature*. He also refereed many papers and reviewed many books. It was a pleasure to review good work but when necessary he did not shirk from giving a book a trouncing.

An instance was *Practical Physics, Molecular Physics and Sound* by Frederick Guthrie, Professor of Physics at the Normal School of Science, Kensington. James thought that Guthrie had done harm by giving readers the jargon of science without the substance, and he pulled no punches in his review for *Nature*[6]. But he felt sorry for Guthrie; the chap had been doing his best, albeit misguidedly, and to get a public mauling from a heavyweight like Maxwell was a humiliation. Three weeks later, *Nature* published a remarkably cheerful letter from Guthrie. 'Some well-meaning friend has sent me a copy of the inclosed. There appear to be various opinions as to the authorship. It has even been suggested that Professor Maxwell, with that sense of humour for which he is so esteemed and with a pardonable love of mystification, is himself the author'. The poem followed:

WORRY, through duties Academic,
   It might ha'e been
That made ye write your last polemic
   Sae unco keen:

Or intellectual indigestion
   O' mental meat,
Striving in vain to solve some question
   Fro' 'Maxwell's Heat'.

Mayhap that mighty brain, in glidin'
   Fro' space tae space,
Met with anither, an' collidin'
   Not face tae face,

But rather crookedly, in fallin'
  Wi' gentle list,
Gat what there is nae help fro' callin'
  An ugly twist.

If 'twas your 'demon' led ye blindly,
  Ye should not thank him,
But gripe him by the lug and kindly
  But soundly spank him.

Sae, stern but patronising daddie!
  Don't ta'e't amiss,
If puir castigated laddie
  Observes just this:-

Ye've gat a braw new lab'ratory
  Wi' all the gears,
Fro' which the warld is unco' sorry,
  Maist naught appears.

A weel-bred dog, yoursel' must feel,
  Should seldom bark.
Just put your fore paws tae the wheel,
  An' do some Wark.

The only plausible explanation of this odd but endearing little comedy is that the poem was James' way of showing fellow-feeling with Guthrie, at the same time defusing the tension by poking fun at himself. Guthrie would guess at once who had written the poem but James was implicitly inviting him to be a conspirator in the scheme by sending it to *Nature* with the pretence that he was mystified. Everyone would see through the pretence, but that was part of the joke.

When it came to books for students, James' ideas on how it should be done are nowhere better shown than in a little gem of a book published in 1877, *Matter and Motion*. It deals with the foundations of dynamics, is written in simple, jargon-free language and can be followed by someone who has done a little advanced school mathematics. Yet it is in no way 'dumbed down'; the reader is required to think. It is an aid to true understanding rather than to passing exams or impressing dinner companions with one's knowledge of the jargon. It bears the Maxwell stamp just as surely as do his great theories.

Much of James' time was taken up in dealings with publishers: marking up proofs must have been almost a daily occupation. Like gasmen, they were one of the few sets of people who exhausted his patience. His main complaint was their niggardliness; their guiding rule seemed to be 'A stitch in nine saves time'.

He felt at home amid the buzz and camaraderie of life at Cambridge. When time allowed, he attended a small essay club that was rather like the 'Apostles' club he had belonged to as a student, but composed of middle-aged professors and dons. He relished the free-wheeling discussions and contributed several essays on philosophical themes. In one he dismisses the belief, then widely held, that scientific laws implied a mechanically deterministic universe, in which the future is predictable, and in doing so gives a remarkable statement of the basis of chaos theory, which mathematicians did not begin to develop until 100 years later:

> When the state of things is such that an infinitely small variation of the present state will alter only by an infinitely small quantity the state at some future time, the condition of the system, whether at rest or in motion, is said to be stable; but when an infinitely small variation in the present state may bring about a finite difference in the state of the system in a finite time, the condition of the system is said to be unstable.
>
> It is manifest that the existence of unstable conditions renders impossible the prediction of future events, if our knowledge of the present state is only approximate and not accurate.[7]

—an exact description of the problem faced by today's weather forecasters.

James' colleagues were in no doubt that they had a remarkable man in their midst. Lewis Campbell gives us an idea of the kind of impression he made on them:

> One great charm of Maxwell's society was his readiness to converse on almost any topic with those he was accustomed to meet, although he always showed a certain degree of shyness when introduced to strangers. He would never tire of talking with boyish glee about the devil on two sticks and similar topics, and no one ever talked to him for five minutes without having some perfectly new ideas set before him; some so startling as to utterly confound the listener, but always such as to repay a thoughtful examination.

And he could still never resist a chance to poke a little fun. Sometimes the joke rebounded; Campbell reports:

> On one occasion, after removing a large amount of calcareous deposit which had accumulated in a curiously colitic form in a boiler, Maxwell sent it to the Professor of Geology with a request that he would identify the formation. This he did at once, vindicating his science from the aspersion that his brother professor would playfully have cast on it.

When another of his fellow professors was to be honoured by a portrait which had been specially commissioned from the popular artist Lowes Dickinson by a group of colleagues and admirers, James was ready with a poem to mark the unveiling. The subject of the portrait was the great mathematician Arthur Cayley, who had invented the theory of matrices and the geometry of any number of dimensions. True to form, James managed to evoke the spirit of the occasion—which was a serious and heartfelt tribute to Cayley—and to make a joke of it at the same time:

> O wretched race of men, to space confined!
> What honour can ye pay to him, whose mind
> To that which lies beyond hath penetrated?
> The symbols he hath formed shall sound his praise,
> And lead him on in unimagined ways
> To conquests new, in worlds not yet created.
>
> . . .
>
> March on symbolic host! with step sublime,
> Up to the flaming bounds of Space and Time!
> There pause, until by Dickinson depicted,
> In two dimensions, we the form may trace
> Of him whose soul, too large for vulgar space,
> In *n* dimensions flourished unrestricted.[8]

James' personal influence in Cambridge spread far beyond his own department. Many mathematicians made use of his ideas and suggestions in their own work. People who were at first hostile to the new Laboratory, with its emphasis on combining theory with practical work, were, in time, completely disarmed by his unaffected charm and patent generosity of spirit. Science at Cambridge entered a new age.

Nor was his influence confined to Cambridge, Britain, or even Europe. He always found time to encourage young scientists and could spot talent at any distance. Among those whose careers he boosted were the outstanding Americans Josiah Willard Gibbs and Henry Rowland, whose own countrymen were slow to recognise their abilities. The way he helped Rowland was especially characteristic.

In his early 20s Rowland was the first person to find a rigorous magnetic analogy to Ohm's law but had his work repeatedly rejected by the *American Journal of Science*. Exasperated, he sent his paper across the Atlantic to Maxwell, who saw its merit at once, had it published in the *Philosophical Magazine*, and wrote back with congratulations and suggestions. When Rowland applied for a professorship at the new Johns Hopkins University in Baltimore, he showed his correspondence with Maxwell to the University President, who thought it 'worth more than a whole stack of recommendations' and gave him the job. Hearing that Rowland was to make a working tour of Europe starting that summer, James invited him to Glenlair. There they mulled over an idea for an experiment to show that a moving electric charge generated magnetic effects like those of a current in a wire. The following year, in Berlin, Rowland approached the august Helmholtz, asking for space in his superbly equipped laboratory to do the experiment. Helmholtz was reluctant, as the place was already bustling with high quality research, but once again Maxwell's interest served as the strongest possible recommendation and the great professor decided to give the young American a basement room. The ambitious experiment used a rapidly spinning ebonite disc, a beam of light and a delicately suspended mirror. It succeeded magnificently. James was delighted for his young friend and celebrated the exploit in inimitable fashion with a poem:

The mounted disc of ebonite
  Has whirled before, nor whirled in vain;
Rowland of Troy, that doughty knight,
  Convection currents did obtain
In such a disc, of power to wheedle,
From its loved north the subtle needle.

'Twas when Sir Rowland, as a stage
  From Troy to Baltimore, took rest
In Berlin, there old Archimage,
  Armed him to follow up this quest;
Right glad to find himself possessor
Of the irrepressible Professor.

But wouldst thou twirl that disc once more,
  Then follow in Childe Rowland's train,
To where in busy Baltimore
  He brews the bantlings of his brain ...

Presumably, the association of Rowland's name with the legends of Charlemagne and the fact he hailed from Troy (in New York State) was enough to send James into mock-epic mode. Goodness knows what Rowland made of it, but Maxwell's bit of fun brought him well-merited publicity and he became America's best-known physicist. He never shook off the epithet 'the doughty knight of Baltimore'.

Although he was not himself a prolific inventor of technical devices, James was an enthusiastic admirer of inventors such as Charles Wheatstone, William Thomson, David Hughes, Thomas Edison and Alexander Graham Bell. When asked to give a public lecture in 1878, he chose to talk about the technological wonder of the day—Bell's invention, the telephone. In typically whimsical fashion, he wove a picture of the telephone as a symbol of the cross-fertilisation of different sciences. One such science was elocution, the speciality of Graham Bell's father, Alexander Melville Bell. Addressing the company in strong Gallowegian tones, James spoke of the elder Bell:

> ... his whole life has been employed in teaching people to speak. He brought the art to such perfection that, though a Scotchman, he taught himself in six months to speak English, and I regret extremely that when I had the opportunity in Edinburgh I did not take lessons from him.

The heavy new commitments naturally took their toll on the quantity of James' own creative work, but not on the quality: his intellectual élan and originality were as evident as ever.

His *Treatise on Electricity and Magnetism* is probably, after Newton's *Principia*, the most renowned book in the history of physics[9]. It was published in 1873 and has been in continuous use ever since. In 1000 pages of crisply written text and mathematics it encompasses virtually everything that was known about electricity and magnetism. It has inspired most of the work done in the subject ever since. At first glance it looks like a text book; indeed, most modern texts are ultimately derived from it, although they often fail to match its clarity. But a closer

look shows it to be something far more interesting. Sometimes Maxwell takes you along a path to a certain point, then, when you expect to go on, takes you back to the start and along a new path which leads to areas inaccessible from the first. The book is not an atlas but an explorer's report. James had written it for himself as well as for others—to consolidate his own knowledge as a base for further exploration. He had begun an extensive revision of the *Treatise* at the time of his early death.

In the *Treatise* James made an important new prediction from his electromagnetic theory—that electromagnetic waves exert a radiation pressure. Bright sunlight, he calculated, presses on the earth's surface with a force of around 4 pounds per square mile, equivalent to 7 grams per hectare. This was too tiny a value to be observable in everyday life and its detection posed a challenge to experimenters. Eventually, in 1900, the Russian physicist Pyotr Lebedev succeeded, and confirmed James' prediction. Although small on an earthly scale, radiation pressure is one of the factors that shape the universe. Without it there would be no stars like our sun—it is internal radiation pressure that stops them from collapsing under their own gravity. James' discovery also helped to explain a phenomenon that had puzzled astronomers for centuries—why comets' tails point away from the sun[10].

He extended other aspects of his electromagnetic theory in the *Treatise* and, where possible, gave practical applications: for example, he explained the principles to be followed when correcting compass readings on iron ships and referred to the Admiralty manual on the subject. He also introduced quaternion notation into the electromagnetic field equations, making them look much like they do in our modern vector notation. But knowing that the compact new quaternion format would look strange to most readers, he included the old cartesian (x, y, z) format equations as well. One outcome of this was that he ran out of letters, having used up the entire Roman and Greek alphabets. He resorted to Roman letters in German Gothic script for his new variables, with the result that the quaternion equations in the *Treatise* have a strange Wagnerian aura.

James' enthusiastic follower Ludwig Boltzmann had published two superb papers on gas theory in 1868 and 1872. Taking James' idea of the velocity distribution of molecules in a gas, he had derived a more general law for their energy distribution—now known as the Maxwell–Boltzmann distribution. He had also generalised James' principle for the equipartition of energy, showing that it should be divided equally not only between modes of linear and rotational movement but among all the independent components of motion in the system.

James had inspired Boltzmann; now he was inspired in turn. The new results were wonderful, even though he found the writing rather long-winded—he re-derived Boltzmann's main result for *Nature* on a single page. James responded with a masterful paper: *On Boltzmann's Theorem on the Average Distribution of Energy in a System of Material Points*. This work, more than any other, laid the foundations for the development by Boltzmann and others of statistical mechanics—an esoteric but useful subject which enables physicists to explain the properties of matter in terms of the behaviour, *en masse*, of its molecules. He derived the velocity and energy distributions in a powerful new way, which gave the equipartition principle as a by-product. One of the key ideas in the paper was what came to be called the method of ensemble averaging, in which the actual system under study is replaced by a statistically equivalent arrangement that is much easier to analyse. The highly mathematical analysis concluded with a practical application directly from the theory: gaseous mixtures could be separated by means of a centrifuge. Many years later this became a standard commercial technique.

One big problem remained. Maxwell and Boltzmann's theory still predicted a different value for the ratio of the specific heats of air at constant pressure and at constant volume from that measured in experiments[11]. In fact, things were getting worse. From the new technique of spectroscopy developed by Kirchhoff and Bunsen came evidence that gas molecules could vibrate as well as rotate. When this effect was allowed for, the ratio of specific heats predicted by the theory was even further from the observed value.

James could not explain the discrepancy and was not convinced by various ingenious attempts by Boltzmann. Summing up the situation in *Nature*, he concluded that 'something essential to the complete statement of the physical theory of molecular encounters must have hitherto escaped us' and that the only thing to do was to adopt the attitude of 'thoroughly conscious ignorance that is the prelude to every real advance in science'.

He was right, as usual. The explanation came 50 years later from quantum theory. By the equipartition principle, Maxwell and Boltzmann's theory held that in the course of billions of molecular collisions kinetic energy is exchanged between all the different modes of motion—linear, rotational and vibrational—so that everything evens out. If energy were infinitely divisible gases would indeed behave this way, but, as we now know, energy can only be exchanged in discrete packets, or quanta. And the quantum size is different for each mode of motion, the vibrational quanta being the largest. In very hot air many of the molecular collisions are violent enough to supply the quanta of energy needed to start the nitrogen and oxygen molecules vibrating, but at lower temperatures most of the collisions are too feeble for this to happen and so vibrational modes are 'frozen' out of the exchanges and play no part in the specific heat. At lower temperatures still, the rotational modes are also frozen out. In consequence of all this, the ratio of the specific heats at constant pressure and constant volume depends on a complex set of interacting factors, rather than on the simple formula James and Boltzmann had been using.

In 1874 William Crookes caused a sensation with his 'radiometer'—a toy-like device that seemed to work by magic. It was a little paddle wheel with blades silvered on one side and blackened on the other, inside a glass bulb from which most of the air had been pumped out. When exposed to light or radiant heat the paddle wheel turned. The public and scientists alike were fascinated. No one could explain how it worked.

The mystery deepened when it became clear that Maxwell's radiation pressure was *not* what drove the wheel: the force on the paddle blades was much too large and in the wrong direction! Scientists everywhere made their own radiometers and tried all manner of design variations in the search for clues. There were various speculative theories but the first real breakthrough was made by James' friend P. G. Tait and his colleague James Dewar (who had discovered the element thallium and later invented the vacuum flask). Crookes had pumped out as much air as he could from the glass bulb but Tait and Dewar found that the radiometer effect depended on the small amount which was left behind. But still nobody knew how the remaining trace of rarefied gas drove the paddle wheel.

James now entered the arena. He applied his kinetic theory of gases but at first all he got was an apparently elegant proof that the gas in the bulb would quickly reach a stable temperature distribution so there would be no resultant force on the paddle blades. Then he realised that the gas must be acting on the part of the blades he had so far neglected—the edges. Convection currents from the hotter (blackened) to the cooler (silvered) sides would move along the blades and around the edges, where the gas molecules would interact with the surfaces and transfer some of their momentum to the paddle wheel. At very low gas pressures these 'slip' currents would become the dominant effect.

He embodied these findings in a much more general discussion in a paper for the Royal Society, *On Stresses in Rarefied Gases Arising from Inequalities of Temperature*, putting forward the slip current effect as an explanation of the paddle wheel's movement but giving no formula for it. Here things might have stayed, but William Thomson, who refereed the paper, nudged him into trying to quantify the effect. James came up with a remarkably simple and useful formula based on the assumption that a fraction f of the gas molecules is absorbed by the surface and later evaporated off, while the remaining fraction $(1 - f)$ is reflected—the value of f depending on the type of gas and the type of surface. He issued this result and others in an appendix to the paper. It was his last published work, as the illness which was to take his life was by now asserting its grip.

As things turned out, James' paper did not solve the puzzle of the radiometer. But it did something far more significant by creating the science of rarefied gas dynamics, on which our knowledge of the upper atmosphere depends, and launching a vast body of research on gas-surface effects.

The search for the secret of Crookes' little radiometer generated discoveries and advances out of all proportion to its intrinsic importance. The biggest benefit of all turned out to be the improvement, led by Crookes himself, in the design of vacuum pumps. The ability to set up and maintain very low gas densities made possible many discoveries of the late nineteenth and early twentieth centuries, including that of the electron.

Martin Goldman reports a final twist to the radiometer story in *The Demon in the Aether*. The definitive solution to the puzzle was given in the 1920s by Chapman and Cowling. They showed that there is, after all, a force on the blades which would be sufficient to turn the paddle even if the slip current effect did not exist. Maxwell had made an incorrect simplification in his initial equations, which invalidated his conclusions about the radiometer but not his more general results. The irony is that had he not made this mistake he might have ignored the slip current effect altogether and his pioneering '*f*' formula would have had to wait for another inventor.

While James was working on this paper he was asked by the Royal Society's secretary, George Gabriel Stokes, to referee one by Osborne Reynolds which covered some of the same ground. This was awkward but as the papers differed in their main substance he decided that he could fairly referee Reynolds' paper without holding back his own. Reynolds had made some errors but James thought the conclusions were broadly correct and recommended that it be published 'after the author has had the opportunity to make certain improvements in it'. That done, he completed his own paper, which included a generous tribute to Reynolds. Meanwhile, Reynolds' paper was delayed further by Thomson, the other referee, whose comments were vehemently critical. When James' paper came out first Reynolds was livid. It seemed to him that the great Maxwell had played foul and he complained angrily to Stokes. His letter drew a stinging reply. Stokes was a good friend of James, who by this time was critically ill, and he rebuked Reynolds for what he saw as boorish behaviour. This served only to fuel poor Reynolds' resentment. Had James lived longer he would probably have found a way to dispel the unpleasantness. As it was, Reynolds was probably the only person ever to harbour a grudge against him. Reynolds went on to do excellent work on the theory of fluids and is commemorated by the Reynolds number, which determines when fluid flow changes from smooth to turbulent.

At Cambridge the Maxwells lived at Scroope Terrace, a short walk from the Laboratory. Although the circumstances were similar, home life there was different from that in Kensington 10 years before. There were no home experiments, as James now had the grand new laboratory nearby. And his work responsibilities were much heavier; they could no longer go riding every afternoon. There was another change; Katherine began to suffer from poor health. She felt weak for much of the time and often needed nursing. James would sit with her while working on his manuscripts. For one 3 week spell he did got go to bed but slept in a chair at her bedside—yet worked with his usual energy during the day. Perhaps because of her illness, the cause of which was never found, she seems not to have been very welcoming to James' colleagues and some of them took a dislike to her. To spare either her or his colleagues distress, James sometimes conducted business at the laboratory which might have been more congenially done over a cup of tea at home.

We know very little of Katherine directly but she has acquired a reputation among Maxwell aficionados as a 'difficult' woman. Some harsh views about her have been attributed to Mrs Tait and to some of James' female relations. His cousin Jemima Blackburn reports in her memoirs that Katherine was 'neither pretty, nor healthy, nor agreeable' and had 'a jealous and suspicious nature'.

But perhaps twentieth century writers have made too much of such criticism. Mrs Tait was not the most reliable of witnesses: she used to say that Katherine tried to stop Maxwell's scientific work, which is clearly nonsense. And there was a callous streak in cousin Jemima's make-up: when her nephew and staunch friend Colin Mackenzie died in 1881 she kept her family away from the funeral because of rumours that he had been involved in some scandal. Colin was also a good friend to the Maxwells and has a further part to play in our story. Katherine was certainly no impediment to Maxwell's continued friendship with Colin and with his other male cousins William and Charles Cay, who were regular visitors to Glenlair. One strong sign of mutual regard was that Katherine named her pony after Charles[12].

Whether or not Katherine deserves her reputation, it is clear that the marriage did not escape its share of tension. It is also clear that they were loyally devoted to one another, with a strong spiritual sense of union, that they always shared their deepest thoughts, and that James always put Katherine's welfare before his own.

They spent about 4 months of each year at Glenlair. This gave James a chance to catch up with local developments and to fulfil his duties as Laird and as a leading citizen of the area. Riding was still their favourite exercise. Lewis Campbell reports the recollections of a neighbour:

> Mr Ferguson remembers him in 1874, on his new black horse, 'Dizzy', which had been the despair of previous owners, 'riding the ring', for the amusement of the children at Kilquhanity, throwing up his whip and catching it, leaping over bars, etc.

At Glenlair, local issues had first call on his attention. It was at this time that James had his long-running losing battle with the economy-minded School Board who wanted to close the school at Merkland. But he also kept the postman busy emptying and replenishing the post box in the wall at the end of his drive. Many of his papers and articles were written at Glenlair, and he kept in touch with people who were working over the vacations at the Cavendish, advising on experiments.

As the end of the decade approached, James had reason to be pleased with the way things were going. He had not sought the post at the Cavendish but it had become an important part of his life. He took immense pride in the work of his young researchers. The Laboratory had confounded the sceptics and had generated a great swell of interest in science at Cambridge. His own theoretical ideas were still developing, and now that the great labour on the Henry Cavendish papers was finished he would have more time to pursue them. He enjoyed the variety and balance of his working life and interests: town and country, science and people, experiments and mathematics. And the curiosity about everything in the physical world which had driven him as a child to fire fusillades of 'What's the go o' that?' questions at his indulgent parents burned as strongly as ever. Maturity had honed his skill and strengthened his judgement without in any way dulling his freshness or enthusiasm. But the disease that had shortened his mother's life struck again. The 1880s had promised to be fruitful years, but he did not live to see them.

CHAPTER ELEVEN

LAST DAYS

In the spring of 1877 James had begun to suffer from heartburn. He found that sodium bicarbonate relieved the symptoms and for a year and a half continued to run the Laboratory, give his lectures, and write his papers, articles and reviews with apparently undiminished vigour—all the while thinking more about Katherine's health than his own. Then friends and colleagues noticed that his step had lost some of its spring and his eyes some of their sparkle. The bicarbonate became less and less effective at relieving the heartburn and he began to have difficulty swallowing. Uncharacteristically, he turned down a request for a contribution to T. H. Huxley's *English Men of Science*, pleading overwork. In April 1879 he mentioned his symptoms to the family doctor when writing to him about Katherine, and was prescribed milk in place of meat. He continued to give lectures and went to the laboratory to give directions and advice but could only stay a short time each day.

In June he and Katherine went to Glenlair as usual. By September he was getting attacks of violent pain but insisted on going ahead with a planned visit by William Garnett, his demonstrator at the Cavendish, and his wife[1]. Garnett was alarmed by the change in his appearance but marvelled at the way he still conducted evening prayers for the whole household and at the care he bestowed on his guests. He showed them memorabilia of his childhood: the oval curves, cousin Jemima's water colours, the bagpipes that had saved his grandfather's life. When they walked round the estate he went with them a little way down to the river, pointing out where the stepping stones used to be and where he used to bathe and sail in the old washtub. This was the longest walk he had taken for some weeks. When they went for a drive in the afternoon he could not go with them because the shaking of the carriage was unbearably painful.

He remembered his mother's torment and must have been fairly certain that he was suffering from the same disease. To get an authoritative diagnosis they sent for Professor Sanders from Edinburgh. He arrived on 2 October and, finding that it was indeed an advanced case of abdominal cancer, told James that he had about a month to live. Sanders urged James to go to Cambridge, where Dr Paget would be able to arrange relief for the worst of the pain and help to make his last few weeks as bearable as possible for Katherine as well as himself. Luckily Katherine was having a period of respite from her own illness and was able to organise the packing and the journey.

On arrival in Cambridge on 8 October, James was so weak he could barely walk from the train to a carriage. Once in the care of Dr Paget, his pain was considerably relieved and for a few days he seemed slightly better. The news spread and some of his friends felt a frisson of hope that he would recover, but then his remaining strength began to ebb away and it was clear to everyone that he was dying.

Dr Paget later described this time:

> As he had been in health, so was he in sickness and in the face of death. The calmness of his mind was never once disturbed. His sufferings were acute for some days after his return to Cambridge, and, even after their mitigation, were still of a kind to try severely any ordinary patience and fortitude. But they were never spoken of by him in a complaining tone. In the midst of them his thoughts and consideration were rather for others than for himself.
>
> Neither did the approach of death disturb his habitual composure ... A few days before his death he asked me how much longer he could last. This inquiry was made with the

> most perfect calmness. He wished to live until the expected arrival from Edinburgh of his friend and relative Mr Colin Mackenzie. His only anxiety seemed to be about his wife, whose health had for a few years been delicate and had recently become worse ...
>
> His intellect also remained clear and apparently unimpaired to the last. While his bodily strength was ebbing away to death, his mind never wandered or wavered, but remained clear to the very end. No man ever met death more consciously or more calmly.

James' local doctor at Glenlair, Dr Lorraine, had sent a note on the case to Dr Paget. This was, of course, routine. What was extraordinary was that Dr Lorraine had such admiration for the patient that he spontaneously included a tribute in his professional note:

> I must say he is one of the best men I have ever met, and a greater merit than his scientific achievements is his being, so far as human judgement can discern, a most perfect example of a Christian Gentleman.

According to Dr Paget, this remark accurately described the feelings of all who knew Maxwell during his last illness. It also bears a striking similarity to comments made independently by various people who had met him over the years.

James' own reflections on his life were typically self-effacing. He told his friend and Cambridge colleague Professor Hort:

> What is done by what I call myself is, I feel, done by something greater than myself in me ...
>
> I have been thinking how very gently I have always been dealt with. I have never had a violent shove in all my life.
>
> The only desire which I can have is like David to serve my own generation by the will of God, and then fall asleep.

James Clerk Maxwell died on 5 November 1879. Katherine and his good friend and cousin Colin Mackenzie were with him. The following Sunday many people attended a memorial service at St Mary's Church, Cambridge. The sense of loss was palpable, and the task of giving it a voice fell to the Rev. H. M. Butler, one of James' old friends from student days who was by now headmaster of Harrow School. He put it simply, with a fitting choice of metaphor:

> It is not often, even in this great home of thought and knowledge, that so bright a light is extinguished as that which is now mourned by many illustrious mourners, here chiefly, but also far beyond this place.[2]

These thoughts were echoed by P. G. Tait, writing in *Nature*:

> I cannot adequately express in words the extent of the loss which his early death has inflicted not merely on his personal friends, on the University of Cambridge, on the whole scientific world, but also, and most especially, on the cause of common sense, of true science, and of religion itself, in these days of much vain-babbling, pseudo-science, and materialism. But men of his stamp never live in vain; and in one sense at least they cannot die. The spirit of Clerk Maxwell still lives with us in his imperishable writings, and will speak to the next generation by the lips of those who have caught inspiration from his teachings and example.

After a preliminary ceremony in Trinity College Chapel, James' body was taken to Glenlair and buried in Parton Churchyard next to that of his father and mother. Katherine was buried there 7 years later and the four share a headstone. At the roadside in front of the church stands a simple plaque. The inscription summarises his career and achievements, and concludes:

> A good man, full of humour and wisdom, he lived in this area and is buried in the ruins of the old Kirk in this Churchyard.

This and a stained glass window in the church at Corsock are the only memorials that a visitor to the area is likely to find. But

there is another. Glenlair passed to the Wedderburn family and the house was destroyed by fire in 1929. If you walk half a mile down a private drive off the Dalbeattie to Corsock road, crossing the Urr by William Dyce Cay's bridge, you will see the shell of a building, its chimneys and roofless gables pointing silently to the sky.

CHAPTER TWELVE

MAXWELL'S LEGACY

The influence of James Clerk Maxwell runs all through our daily lives. His electromagnetic waves bring us radio and television and provide the radar that makes safe air travel possible. Colour television works on the three-colour principle that he demonstrated. Pilots fly aircraft by control systems which derive from his work. Many of our bridges and other structures were designed using his reciprocal diagrams and photoelastic techniques.

Even more significant is his influence on the whole development of physical science. He started a revolution in the way physicists look at the world. It was he who began to think that the objects and forces that we see and feel may be merely our limited perception of an underlying reality which is inaccessible to our senses but may be described mathematically.

He was the first to use field equations to represent physical processes; they are now the standard form used by physicists to model what goes on in the vastness of space and inside atoms. He was also the first to use statistical methods to describe processes involving many particles, another technique which is now standard. He predicted, correctly, that light was a wholly electromagnetic phenomenon and that its speed was simply the ratio between the electromagnetic and electrostatic units of charge. His equations of the electromagnetic field were the chief inspiration for Einstein's special theory of relativity and, along with his kinetic theory of gases, played a part in Planck's discovery of the quantum of energy. His thought experiment,

Maxwell's demon, has been creatively employed in information theory and computer science.

The Cavendish Laboratory, which he designed and started up, has been the site of many discoveries, including the electron and the structure of DNA. It is sometimes said, with no more than slight overstatement, that if you trace every line of modern physical research to its starting point you come back to Maxwell. Professor C. A. Coulson put it another way: 'There is scarcely a single topic that he touched upon which he did not change almost beyond recognition'.

The breathtaking depth and scope of his influence are all the more remarkable because his career was cut short by early death when he was in full flow. Still more remarkable is that he is so little known to the public. Everyone has heard of Newton and Einstein but Maxwell is almost unknown outside professional circles. Why this should be so is indeed a puzzle but there are a number of possible reasons.

The one most often put forward is his modesty. He never strove to promote his own work; nor was there anyone who did it for him, as T. H. Huxley did for Darwin. While true, this is at best a part explanation. During his lifetime Maxwell's main theories had yet to be experimentally verified and he knew from the history of science that even the greatest men had sometimes been wrong. It was not so much his modesty as his philosophical caution that held him back.

Perhaps the foremost reason is that many of his ideas were ahead of their time. The point is best illustrated by his electromagnetic theory. In the 1870s there was scant support for it in Britain outside a small group at Cambridge. It was such a new type of theory that most people were simply baffled. Even some of those who could follow all the mathematics distrusted the theory because it gave no mechanical explanations. They went along with Maxwell's earlier spinning cell model, with all its oddities, but thought that he had gone slightly mad with his dynamical theory. Among these was Maxwell's friend, William Thomson, who was by far the most influential physicist in Britain. Someone who did take the theory seriously was Hermann Helmholtz. He was professor of physics at Berlin University and as powerful in Germany as Thomson was in Britain. In 1879 Helmholtz persuaded the Berlin Academy of Sciences to offer a prize for a conclusive experimental test of Maxwell's theory. His star student, Heinrich Hertz, took up the challenge.

The task was formidable: to produce and detect either displacement currents or electromagnetic waves. Light waves did not serve this purpose. They were easy to detect and, according to Maxwell's theory, electromagnetic, but had frequencies far higher than could be produced directly by any known electrical or magnetic means. Conversely, an oscillating electrical circuit—for example, one containing a rapidly repeated spark discharge—would, if the theory was right, produce waves, but the problem lay in detecting them. Maxwell and his students at the Cavendish had fought shy of such work: it was risky and the first priority for the new Laboratory was to establish a solid reputation.

For 8 years, on and off, Hertz persevered, first as a student, then as professor of physics at Karlsruhe, trying in various ways to detect the smallest signs of a displacement current in insulators. In 1887, he put a block of paraffin between the plates of a capacitor which was rapidly charged and discharged, and looked hopefully for sparks across a small gap in a detector loop. Amazingly, sparks appeared not just in his detector but all over the apparatus. Energy from his rapidly oscillating circuit was, it seemed, being transmitted through the air and reflected by the walls. Never mind the displacement current, here was strong circumstantial evidence of electromagnetic waves; could he do better and find direct proof?

Indeed he could. His brilliant experiment made use of a well-known property of all travelling waves: when reflected back directly towards the source, the forward and backward components combine to create *standing* waves. Since the standing waves appear simply to oscillate in the same place they are much easier to study. Another property of waves is that, for a given travelling speed, wavelength is inversely proportional to frequency; the higher the frequency the shorter the wavelength. Fortuitously, the frequency of Hertz's spark discharge source was high enough to give waves short enough for their length to be measured in the laboratory. Using a metal sheet reflector and a spark-gap detector, Hertz found beautiful standing waves with a wavelength of about 30 centimetres.

Eight years after his death, Maxwell's electromagnetic theory had been emphatically verified. But its significance had scarcely begun to dawn on the scientific community, let alone the public. There was surprisingly little acclaim among British scientists for their countryman's achievement. Even in Cambridge, reaction was muted, perhaps because Hertz had outshone their own efforts.

One can hardly fault the Cavendish for failing to produce an experimenter of the calibre of Hertz but it is a fact that no-one there had made a serious and sustained attempt to confirm Maxwell's theory. It is in no way a criticism to surmise that, had they taken the chance and succeeded, Cambridge would have become established in the public mind as the birthplace of electromagnetic waves and Maxwell as the father. They would have been called not Hertzian waves but Maxwellian.

A few years later, some people who were not established scientists began to have some success in sending and detecting electromagnetic waves. One was a young schoolmaster in Christchurch, New Zealand. When he got a scholarship to England in 1895 to take up research at the Cavendish Laboratory he brought his detector with him. Soon he was sending and detecting waves over a range of half a mile. His name was Ernest Rutherford. But Rutherford rapidly became immersed in other work and lost interest in the waves. One can see why: the Cavendish was a-buzz with exciting experiments on the conduction of electricity through gases and J. J. Thomson was on the threshold of discovering the electron. Rutherford was soon making his own discoveries in that field. Had he been differently inclined, Cambridge might have become the birthplace of radio, with a consequent further boost to Maxwell's public reputation.

A young Italian arrived in Britain at about the same time as Rutherford. Guglielmo Marconi had come specifically to seek support for his experiments on sending and detecting waves, having failed to interest his own countrymen. Helped by an English cousin and by William Preece, chief engineer to the Post Office, he took out patents and extended the range of detection. There was still no commercial interest, so he started his own company and, in a brilliantly successful piece of publicity, equipped two ships to send reports on the 1899 America's Cup yacht race to a shore station, from where they could be telegraphed by cable to newspapers in America and Britain. Wireless telegraphy was born. Sound radio followed, and then television and worldwide communication via satellites.

In the popular account Marconi gets the credit for inventing radio and Hertz for discovering the waves. Maxwell, whose inspired prediction started the whole thing off, is rarely mentioned.

While Marconi was finding ways of putting Maxwell's theory to everyday use, a junior official in the Swiss Patent Office was pondering the fundamental nature of space and time. Albert Einstein brooded over an apparent conflict between Maxwell's equations of the electromagnetic field and Newton's laws of motion. It stemmed from a famous experiment by Albert Abraham Michelson and Edward Morley which suggested that light always appears to travel at exactly the same speed, no matter how fast or in what direction the observer is moving. This seemed to contradict common sense but could be explained if distances and times appeared different to observers travelling at different velocities. A formula for converting the times and distances measured by one observer to those measured by another had been put forward by Hendrik Antoon Lorentz. The extraordinary thing was that the formula seemed to be intrinsic to Maxwell's equations; they worked perfectly under this transformation whereas Newton's laws did not.

Einstein resolved the conflict in his *Special Theory of Relativity* by turning the problem inside out. He took the constancy of the speed of light as a starting point and worked out the consequences. He arrived at Lorentz's formula from a new direction and gave it an entirely new perspective. There were no absolute measures of space or time: all observers in uniform relative motion measured them differently and all their measurements were equally valid. A corollary of this was that Maxwell's equations were *the* basic laws of the physical world. Newton's laws were an approximation which worked well as long as the relative speeds of observers were small compared with that of light. Another corollary was the celebrated equation $E = mc^2$; mass was a simply an immensely concentrated form of stored energy.

Underlying all this was Einstein's axiom that the speed of light was an absolute constant. It was the fundamental characteristic of the universe, nature's gearing between space and time. And it was completely determined by Maxwell's theory: its value was simply the ratio of the electromagnetic and electrostatic units of charge[1].

Even though it ran counter to common intuition, Einstein's theory was more rapidly accepted than Maxwell's had been. It explained perfectly the way atomic particles behaved when they travelled at speeds approaching that of light and accounted for the loss of mass when a radioactive atom decays into two smaller ones. It later provided the basis for nuclear power generation and the atomic bomb. Einstein followed up the *Special Theory* with his *General Theory of Relativity*, which explained gravity as a geometrical property of space and time. Almost nobody among the public understood it but they were captivated by the mystique of 'curved' space–time and Einstein became an international celebrity, everywhere acclaimed as Newton's successor.

General Relativity was from first to last a *field* theory of the kind pioneered by Maxwell. Einstein was fulsome in recognition of Maxwell's crucial contribution and our hero's stock rose still higher with physicists. None of this, however, reached the public.

Maxwell's electromagnetic theory is now recognised as one of the most important of all scientific discoveries. It is at the heart of physics, and shapes our everyday lives. But recognition of its importance has been gradual, cumulative and largely out of the public view. He is a giant figure who remains just out of sight.

What of Maxwell's part in the genesis of quantum theory? The discovery in the early twentieth century that all forms of energy come in discrete packets is probably the most profound shock ever to hit the scientific world. The first rumblings came from Maxwell's and Boltzmann's work on gases in the 1860s and 1870s, when their theory predicted that the kinetic energy of molecules should be equally distributed over all independent modes of motion. This implied a simple formula for the ratio of the specific heats at constant pressure and constant volume, but, as we have seen, values observed in practice obstinately failed to follow the formula. Maxwell's intuition was spot on when he concluded that 'something essential to the complete statement of the physical theory of molecular encounters must have hitherto escaped us'. His view was reinforced when scientists began to put together the combined implications of the kinetic theory of gases, thermodynamics, and Maxwell's electromagnetic theory in the study of so-called 'black body' radiation. Matters came to a head towards the end of the century, when the combined theories seemed to indicate that all the kinetic energy of molecules should long ago have been radiated away, leaving a cold, dead universe[2]. What was missing? Nature seemed to have some hidden mechanism which curtailed radiation at the higher frequencies and so allowed a balance to be reached between the radiation that matter emitted and the radiation it absorbed. The denouement came in 1900: in what he described as 'an act of desperation', Max Planck produced a formula which achieved the desired balance by allowing matter to absorb radiant energy only in discrete amounts, or 'quanta'. At first Planck mistrusted his monstrous creation and so did everyone else. It took the boldness of Albert Einstein to complete the coup in 1905 by asserting that radiation itself comes in discrete packets, now called photons.

Quantum theory has explained why the specific heats of gases do not follow the simple formula which Maxwell and Boltzmann used, why matter does not radiate away all its energy, and many things besides. There is now no doubt whatever that all forms of energy, including radiation, come in quanta. But, according to Maxwell's electromagnetic theory, radiation consists of continuous waves, not discrete packets. Does this mean his equations are wrong? By no means: Maxwell's theory works perfectly at any scale large enough to allow the minute graininess of energy to be averaged out and, even at smaller scales, it underpins such theories as quantum electrodynamics. It holds complete sway in its own domain but Maxwell never claimed or believed that its fields or waves represent ultimate physical reality. In his own words:

> The changes of direction which light undergoes in passing from one medium to another are identical with the deviations of the path of a particle in moving through a narrow space in which intense forces act. This analogy was long believed to be the true explanation of the refraction of light; and we still find it useful in the solution of certain problems, in which we employ it without danger as an artificial method. The other analogy, between light and the vibrations of an elastic medium, extends much farther, but though its importance and fruitfulness cannot be over-estimated, we must recollect that it is founded only on a resemblance in *form* between the laws of light and those of vibrations.

The great physicist James Jeans, writing in 1931, comments that this sounds 'almost like an extract from a lecture on modern wave-mechanics—and a very good one too'. Maxwell's point is equally relevant today. He is, in effect, telling us that although the things we call photons and electrons appear to us to behave sometimes like particles and sometimes like waves, we should not make the mistake of thinking that they *are* either. His view was exactly that later expressed by J. B. S. Haldane, who said: 'My own suspicion is that the universe is not only queerer than we suppose, but queerer than we can suppose'.

Perhaps the most puzzling aspect of Maxwell's relative obscurity is the poverty of official recognition in his own country. Oxford and Edinburgh gave him honorary degrees but he received only two other British awards in his lifetime: a Rumford Medal from the Royal Society of London and a Keith Medal from the Royal Society of Edinburgh. The work thus rewarded was on colour vision, and reciprocal diagrams for engineering structures. Other countries were less reticent: he received honours from New York, Boston, Philadelphia, Amsterdam, Vienna, Göttingen and Pavia.

As the years went by, other countries still seemed to be more generous with tributes than his own. When the Royal Society of London held its tricentenary celebration in 1960, the Queen attended. In her speech she praised a number of famous former Fellows—presumably listed for her by the Society. Inexplicably, Maxwell was not among them. He has been more widely commemorated elsewhere, even in countries without a strong scientific tradition: for example, the governments of Mexico, Nicaragua and San Marino are among those who have issued special postage stamps in his honour.

There are Maxwell devotees around the world. People from many countries still come to visit his burial place at Parton. His work is, even now, the subject of wide and intense study, both by students and by distinguished scientific historians such as Daniel Siegel and Peter Harman.

A small group based in Edinburgh formed the James Clerk Maxwell Foundation in 1977 and in 1993 succeeded in acquiring the house at 14 India Street where he was born. Fittingly, the house is used as a working centre for the mathematical sciences, a place for scientists, engineers and mathematicians from all countries to meet for seminars and courses. One room holds a lovingly presented display of memorabilia.

People who knew Maxwell have left us with more than his scientific achievements. We have a picture of a man who was the kind of friend everyone would love to have: generous, considerate, brave, genial, entertaining, and entirely without vanity or pretence. The friend who knew him best described his character as having 'a grand simplicity': he was the same all the way through and the same to everyone[3].

The deep wholeness of Maxwell's character is as plain in his scientific work as in his personal life. The little boy who never stopped asking 'What's the go o' that?' became the man who changed the way that physicists think about the world and opened the way to vast new regions of knowledge. His place in the grand scheme of things was aptly described by a scientist from the following generation. Oliver Heaviside was an acerbic and cynical man whose criticism could be withering. But when he spoke of Maxwell all world-weariness dropped away and what shone through was pure joy:

> A part of us lives after us, diffused through all humanity—more or less—and through all nature. This is the immortality of the soul. There are large souls and small souls ... That of a Shakespeare or Newton is stupendously big. Such men live the best part of their lives after they are dead. Maxwell is one of these men. His soul will live and grow for long to come, and hundreds of years hence will shine as one of the bright stars of the past, whose light takes ages to reach us.

NOTES

In the main narrative I have tried as far as possible to tell a simple story. This has meant leaving out much that might be useful or interesting to some readers. The Notes are a second port of call for people who need information on sources or want a little more historical or technical detail on particular points. They also shed some interesting sidelights and I hope that all readers will enjoy browsing through these pages. Anyone who wants to go deeper will find some excellent texts in the bibliography.

Books and articles in the bibliography are generally referred to here only by the name of the author or authors but I have given a fuller description where it seems helpful to do so. Dates of the Maxwell publications described in the main narrative are given here where relevant to the context but readers requiring a full list will find it in the Chronology.

Introduction

The Feynman quotation comes from the book by Feynman, Leighton and Sands listed in the biography.

Chapter 1 A country boy

1. Maxwell was born in Edinburgh on 13 June 1831 in his father's house at 14 India Street.
2. At the time of Maxwell's birth, his father's estate was still referred to as Middlebie. Glenlair was the name his parents

gave to their new house and it seems gradually to have come to represent the whole estate. For simplicity I have used the name Glenlair from the start.

3. The title of the 'Under the sea' poem is *The Song of the Atlantic Telegraph Company*. I have given the second of its four verses; it can be found in full in Campbell and Garnett. The poem is set to the tune of a popular song of the time and it came to Maxwell while on his way by train to Glasgow—perhaps its rhythm was evoked by the clickety-click of train wheels passing over joints in the rails.
4. Much of the information about the Clerk and Kay families comes from David Forfar's article, *Generations of Genius*. Both families were economical with male Christian names: most of the male Clerks were John, James or George and most of the Cays were John or Robert.
5. The Edinburgh Academy was a young school. It was founded in 1824 and had quickly established a fine reputation under its first Rector, the Welshman John Williams, who was still serving during Maxwell's time at the school.

Chapter 2 Pins and string

1. Aunt Isabella lived at 31 Heriot Row, which adjoins India Street. To the family, the house was always known as 'Old 31'.
2. Colour plates of many examples of Jemima Blackburn's work, including several watercolours painted at Glenlair, can be found in *Jemima* (Ed. Rob Finley).
3. Maxwell's school friend P. G. Tait was 1 year behind Maxwell at the Edinburgh Academy, even though they were the same age. Maxwell would, in the normal way, have joined Tait's class but its teacher, James Cumming, had such a strong reputation that the class was full. Hence, as reported in the

narrative, Maxwell had to enrol in the class above, where Lewis Campbell was one of his classmates. Maxwell and Tait both left the Academy in 1847 for Edinburgh University.

4. Both Maxwell and Tait's classes were taught mathematics by James Gloag, who apparently wielded the tawse even more fiercely than the other masters, but was passionate in championing mathematics within the school and a highly effective teacher. As Forfar and Pritchard report in their article, *The Remarkable Story of Maxwell and Tait*, Gloag was 'beside himself' when first Tait then Maxwell did so well at Cambridge, and 'considered the credit entirely his own'!
5. Maxwell's oval curves paper was given the accurate but unwieldy title *Observations on Circumscribed Figures having a Plurality of Foci, and Radii of Various Proportions*.
6. Aunt Jane lived at 6 Great Stuart Street, a few minutes walk from Heriot Row.
7. The title of Maxwell's poem marking his farewell to school is *Song of the Edinburgh Academician.*

Chapter 3 Philosophy

1. As Martin Goldman reports in *The Demon in the Aether*, Professors Hamilton and Forbes were implacable enemies. It could hardly be otherwise given Hamilton's mistrust of all mathematics but geometry. They clashed head on in 1838 over the choice of a new mathematics lecturer; Forbes won this one when his candidate Kelland, a Cambridge expert in algebra and the calculus, got the post.
2. Maxwell's remark 'I never try to discourage a man from trying an experiment ... ' was reported by Arthur Schuster, one of his students at the Cavendish Laboratory.
3. Forbes was also a keen mountaineer and spent a lot of time in the Alps, which is probably where his interest in glaciers began.

4. The quotation 'If a child has any latent talent for the study of nature ... ' is from a book review Maxwell wrote for *Nature* in 1879. The subject was *Practical Physics, Molecular Physics and Sound* by Frederick Guthrie. This is also the review that prompted the poem beginning 'Worry through duties academic ... ', which is given Chapter 10.
5. Professor John Wilson, whose classes on moral philosophy Maxwell regarded with disdain, was also known under his pen-name, Christopher North.
6. The type of polarised light Maxwell was experimenting with is plane polarised light. There is another kind—circularly polarised light—in which the wave motion resembles a corkscrew.

General note

The two papers published at this time were *On the Theory of Rolling Curves* (1848) and *On the Equilibrium of Elastic Solids* (1850).

Chapter 4 Learning to juggle

1. Maxwell's views on 'the dark sciences' were expressed in a letter to his friend R. B. Litchfield.
2. I have abridged the poem about John Alexander Frere, giving the first and the last two verses of seven. The full version can be found in Campbell and Garnett.
3. Charles Babbage's main collaborators in bringing Cambridge University mathematics up to date in the early 1800s were George Peacock, Edward Bromhead and John Herschel, son of the renowned astronomer William Herschel. The breakthrough came in 1817 when Peacock, aged 25, was appointed examiner for the Mathematical Tripos. He set questions using the continental notation for the calculus, which was much

more versatile than the traditional Newtonian notation and quickly became the standard form.

4. William Hopkins was the most successful Cambridge tutor of the time. In a period of about 20 years he coached over 200 wranglers, 17 of whom were senior wranglers. And he managed to drill his students without stifling their creativity. Among their number were George Gabriel Stokes, William Thomson, P. G. Tait, E. J. Routh and Arthur Cayley, who invented the theory of matrices and the geometry of *n* dimensions. Hugh Blackburn, who married Maxwell's artist cousin Jemima, was also a pupil of Hopkins.
5. The friend whose family Maxwell was visiting when he fell ill was G. W. H. Tayler, afterwards Vicar of Holy Trinity, Carlisle. The quotation 'Let each member of the family be allowed ...' comes from a letter to R. B. Litchfield.

Chapter 5 Blue and yellow make pink

1. Helmholtz was ennobled and added the 'von' to his name in 1882. As this is after the time of our story, he appears throughout the narrative as plain Hermann.
2. In describing the colour-mixing experiments of Forbes and Maxwell, I have for simplicity omitted the point that white and grey are, technically speaking, the same colour; they differ only in brightness. White may be thought of as a very bright grey. Progressively reducing the brightness gives light grey, dark grey and, ultimately, black. To show that a particular combination of colours on the outer part of the disc gave white, one needed to match them against a mixture of black and white on the inner part, so that the whole disc appeared the same shade of grey.
3. Thomas Young suggested a triangle for representing colour vision about 50 years before Maxwell. But the idea was

neglected or rejected by many experts before Maxwell took it up. Forbes had tried using a triangle but could not get it to work because he persisted with red, blue and *yellow* as primaries. It was Maxwell who demonstrated the validity of the colour triangle and gave it proper mathematical expression.

4. Maxwell's colour triangle is shown here in the form which I think will be clearest to non-specialist readers. An alternative way is to represent a colour as the weighted sum of three vectors formed by joining any point outside the triangle to each vertex, the weights being the proportional amounts of each primary which make up the colour. The position of the tip of the resultant vector gives the composition of the colour. In this method, the triangle need not be equilateral.
5. The paper on colour vision which Maxwell sent to the Royal Society of Edinburgh in 1855 was *Experiments on Colour, as Perceived by the Eye*.
6. Helmholtz and Maxwell independently discovered the fact that mixing lights is additive, whereas mixing pigments is subtractive. Helmholtz was first to publish but at this stage he had not accepted the three-colour theory; in fact, he explicitly rejects it in his paper. Everitt, in *Maxwell's Scientific Papers*, Applied Optics, Vol. 6, No. 4 (1967), gives the opinion that 'Maxwell and Forbes deserve more credit, and Helmholtz and Grassmann less credit, than is usually given them for the revival of Young's three-component theory of colour vision'.
7. Strictly speaking, there are no such things as magnetic poles, only states of polarisation at individual points. Some physics texts avoid poles altogether. But we are so accustomed to thinking of the earth's north and south poles that it would seem perverse to take the purist's line here, especially as today's electrical engineers use poles all the time as a convenient device for thinking and calculation. The idea of using (fictitious) poles in this way was first proposed by the British astronomer John Michell in 1750. It has the

advantage of making the equations laws of static magnetism identical to those of electrostatics.

8. Newton's letter, 'That gravity should be innate, inherent, and essential to matter ... ', was written to Richard Bentley. The widespread distortion of Newton's views seems to have come from two sources. The first was his own famous statement, 'Hypotheses non fingo'—'I do not frame hypotheses', which was open to misunderstanding. The second was his disciple and evangelist Roger Cotes, who wrote in a preface to Newton's *Principia* that 'action at a distance is one of the primary properties of matter'.
9. The quotation 'Faraday ... shows us his unsuccessful as well as his successful experiments ... ' is from Maxwell's *Treatise on Electricity and Magnetism.*
10. Maxwell's tubes of electric flux differ in one way from those of magnetic flux. The tubes of electric flux always terminate at each end in a charged body. An iron magnet produces tubes of magnetic flux which appear to terminate at its north and south external surfaces but the tubes actually extend into the body of the magnet and join up, forming continuous loops. The difference arises because positive and negative electrical charges can exist separately, whereas magnetic poles come only in north–south pairs, like the heads and tails sides of a coin. An iron magnet can be thought of as many tiny magnets joined end to end; in fact the micro-magnets are the atoms themselves and their magnetism is generated by the orbital motion and spin of their electrons. This explanation that magnetism in permanent magnets is due to tiny circulating electric charges was a brilliant conjecture by Ampère in 1823, which Maxwell and others adopted as a working hypothesis and was borne out by twentieth century findings on atomic structure.
11. The geometrical derivation of the inverse square law of electrical and magnetic forces from Maxwell's analogy can be visualised by imagining fluid flowing uniformly in all

directions from a point source. As the fluid is incompressible, the amount of it emerging per unit time from any sphere centred on the point will be the same, whatever the size of the sphere. It follows that the fluid moves outwards at a rate inversely proportional to the square of its distance from the source, and, by analogy, that electrical and magnetic forces follow the same law.

12. George Green probably died from a lung condition brought on by years of inhaling flour dust in his mill, although the cause was recorded as influenza. Less is known about Green than about any other great British mathematician or scientist, but enthusiasts have recently had his mill in Nottingham restored as a working museum and a biography by Mary Cannell was published in 1993. It is listed in the bibliography.
13. George Green's now famous *Essay on the Application of Mathematical Analysis to the Theories of Electricity and Magnetism* made no impact when published by Green at his own expense in Nottingham in 1828. William Thomson arranged for it to be re-published in the Berlin-based *Journal für die Reine und Angewandte Mathematik*, commonly called Crelle's Journal, after its editor. Crelle published it, in English, in three parts in 1850, 1852 and 1854.
14. Stokes' theorem, a companion to Green's theorem in current texts on vector analysis, was set by Stokes as a Smith's Prize problem in Maxwell's year but he may not be its originator. When Maxwell wanted to include it, with proper billing, in his *Treatise* years later, neither Stokes nor anyone else could remember who had thought of it first. Historians subsequently found it in a letter dated 1850 from Thomson to Stokes, so perhaps it should rightfully be called Thomson's, or Kelvin's, theorem.
15. The quantity which Maxwell defined mathematically and identified with Faraday's electrotonic state is now usually called by the name he later gave it, the 'vector potential'. Its rate of spatial variation at a point in space (in mathematical

terms, its 'curl') gives the magnetic flux density at the point and any change in it with time gives rise to an electromotive force. The latter characteristic gave Maxwell a starting point for his thoughts on how to deal with changing fields.

16. Maxwell published *On Faraday's Lines of Force* in two parts. The first dealt with separate static electrical and magnetic fields. The second, which was more mathematical, dealt with the way steady electric currents and magnetism were related, and included the expression for Faraday's electrotonic state.

17. Faraday's letter to Maxwell was dated 25 March 1857. The full text can be found in Martin Goldman's biography of Maxwell, *The Demon in the Aether*.

18. After a Ray Club meeting, at which his friend Pomeroy had given a talk on the position of the British nation in India, Maxwell wrote to his father. The letter contains one of Maxwell's very few recorded comments on a political subject:

    > ... We seem to be in the position of having undertaken the management of India at the most critical period, when all the old institutions and religions must break up, and yet it is by no means plain how new civilisation and self-government among people so different from us is to be introduced. One thing is clear, that if we neglect them, or turn them adrift again, or simply make money of them, then we must look to Spain and the Americans for our examples of wicked management and consequent ruin.

    Maxwell felt sure that his friend was exactly the type of man to help bring enlightened government to India. Pomeroy joined the British Civil Service there the following year but, as reported in Chapter 6, died bravely in tragic circumstances during the Indian Mutiny.

19. We can get some idea of the nature and intensity of the emotional attachment between Lizzie and Maxwell from an

episode that Lizzie's daughter described to Francis Everitt. Apparently, Lizzie fell into a depression when Maxwell died and her husband was so furious that he seized and burned about 60 letters which Maxwell had written to her long ago, full of discussions of his philosophical opinions. Everitt has drawn my attention to a wry remark by Sydney Smith that takes on an unusual poignancy here: 'In Scotland they even make love metaphysically'.

20. The letter containing the quoted passage, 'At present I confine myself to lucky Nightingale's line of business ...' was to Cecil Monro. Campbell and Garnett give a fuller version.
21. The rival candidate for the Aberdeen post who asked for, and got, a reference from Maxwell was William Swan, later Professor of Natural Philosophy at St Andrews.

General notes

The history of the discovery of the principles of colour vision, from Newton to Maxwell and his contemporaries, is interesting but rather confusing. Helpful accounts which assess Maxwell's work in this context are given by Everitt (both entries in the bibliography) and by Harman.

Maxwell designed a number of useful devices which I have not described in this book, for fear of producing a catalogue rather than a story. One was the platometer referred to in his letter to Monro. Another was a general purpose educational aid on optical instruments; a third was a stereoscope which produced a real image and was easier to use than the more usual virtual image type.

Chapter *6* Saturn and statistics

1. The passage 'It is in personal union with my friends ... ' comes from a long letter to R. B. Litchfield. Campbell and Garnett give the full text.

2. Maxwell's Saturn paper was called *On the Stability of the Motion of Saturn's Rings*.
3. I have quoted the last four of eight verses of *To K. M. D.* and the first and last of four verses of *Will you come along with me?* Campbell and Garnett give the poems in full.
4. James' and Katherine's observations to determine the proportions in which primary colours have to be mixed to match pure spectral colours were reported in *On the Theory of Compound Colours, and the Relations of the Colours of the Spectrum*, which he sent to the Royal Society in 1860. They were using the second version of the colour box. The one used later in London and at Glenlair was the third and final version.
5. The quotation 'If you travel at 17 miles per minute ... ' is from a letter to P. G. Tait. The letter is in the Cambridge University Archive.
6. For simplicity, I have expressed the second statement in Maxwell's derivation of the distribution of molecular velocities as though the velocity components x, y and z and speed s took discrete values. As they can, in fact, vary continuously, a formal version of the statement would refer not to numbers of molecules with particular values of x, y, z and s, but to numbers with values within the infinitesimal ranges x to $x + \mathrm{d}x$, y to $y + \mathrm{d}y$, z to $z + \mathrm{d}z$ and s to $s + \mathrm{d}s$.
7. The account of Adolphe Quetelet's work, which Maxwell recalled having read about 9 years earlier, was by John Herschel. It had been published in the *Edinburgh Review* in 1850. We are greatly in the debt of Francis Everitt, who established the important connection with Herschel and Quetelet and reported it in *James Clerk Maxwell, Physicist and Natural Philosopher*, although Everitt has told me that credit is also due to Charles Gillispie, Stephen Brush and Ted Porter. The method of least squares was originally derived, independently, by Karl Friedrich Gauss and Adrien-Marie Legendre.
8. Maxwell's 1860 paper on gas theory was called *Illustrations of the Dynamical Theory of Gases*.

General note

Much of the information about Maxwell's time in Aberdeen comes from the articles by R. V. Jones and John S. Reid. I am particularly grateful to John Reid for the information about Maxwell's work in Marischal College and to R. V. Jones for the story about the Music Hall dividends.

Chapter 7 Spinning cells

1. The Maxwells lived at 8 Palace Gardens, now number 16, a newly built four storey house rented from the Church Commissioners. It is close to Kensington Gardens, which adjoin Hyde Park.
2. The Playfair cipher was invented by Charles Wheatstone but named after Lyon Playfair, the chemistry professor who took up politics and was made a baron. Playfair promoted the British government's use of Wheatstone's coding system in the mid-nineteenth century. It was easy to use but more secure than earlier systems because the letters in the message to be sent were coded in pairs. When code-breakers became more expert it had to be replaced by more complex ciphers.
3. The lines beginning 'There are powers and thoughts within us ...' are from *Recollections of Dreamland*, written in 1856 at Cambridge. The full poem can be found in Campbell and Garnett.
4. The quotation 'I believe there is a department of the mind conducted independently of consciousness ...' is from a letter to R. B. Litchfield, written in 1857.
5. See Note 7, Chapter 5, about magnetic poles.
6. Maxwell's calculations of the spring stiffness of the cells involved two types of elasticity: resistance to twisting and resistance to compression. It was the ratio between the two which could vary over a factor of 3.

General notes

For simplicity, the main narrative does not describe fully the way that the characteristics of Maxwell's spinning cell model developed in the course of the work. He tried to keep the model as general as possible, introducing specific features at each stage as needed. In Part 1 of *On Physical Lines of Force* he described the rotating elements in his model as 'molecular vortices' in a fluid medium. By Part 3 they had become quasi-solid 'cells' with elastic properties and had taken on spherical form. His mathematical analysis was extraordinarily imaginative, even by Maxwell standards. To investigate the stresses in the medium he used portions which were large enough for the action of the tiny cells within to be treated in aggregate but small enough to be themselves treated as infinitesimal elements in the setting up of differential equations.

Despite the novelty of its ideas, the general thrust of *On Physical Lines of Force* was clear, thanks largely to Maxwell's consummate prose. But some details were harder to interpret. In Part 3, for example, he seemed to make an error in sign in one equation and then to correct for it in another by changing the meaning of one of his symbols from the force exerted by the particles on the cells to the equal and opposite force exerted by the cells on the particles. The matter is still debated by scholars. Daniel M. Siegel makes an illuminating contribution in his book *Innovation in Maxwell's Electromagnetic Theory*.

Chapter 8 The beautiful equations

1. Maxwell reported the results of his home experiment on gas viscosity in *On the Viscosity or Internal Friction of Air and Other Gases*, published in 1866.
2. Faraday was not quite the first to discover that electricity is generated by changing the amount of magnetic flux passing

through a conducting loop. Joseph Henry, then a teacher in Albany, New York State, doing research in his spare time, made the same discovery a few months earlier but did not publish until after hearing of Faraday's results. As the main narrative reports, Henry made the world's first powerful electromagnet and invented the electromagnetic relay. He could have made a fortune from patents on such devices but, like Faraday, had strong religious convictions and spurned wealth. During 32 years as the first Director of the Smithsonian Institution he refused any increase in salary.

3. The results of the experiment to produce a standard of resistance were included in a report to the British Association for the Advancement of Science's Committee on Electrical Standards in 1863. Maxwell's and Jenkin's paper recommending a complete system of units, in which Maxwell introduced the dimensional notation, also appeared in this report, and was reprinted, with revisions, in the *Philosphical Magazine* in 1865.

4. Einstein's use of the tensor calculus, without which he could not have formulated the general theory of relativity, came about through his friend Marcel Grossmann. Grossmann, who was a pure mathematician, spotted the relevance of the earlier work of Levi-Civita and Ricci, and introduced Einstein to it. Levi-Civita and Ricci had developed their methods from the work of Riemann and Christoffel, who, in turn, had built on the ideas of Karl Friedrich Gauss.

5. As the narrative reports, Maxwell made use of Lagrange's method of setting up equations for dynamical systems in his paper *A Dynamical Theory of the Electromagnetic Field*. An alternative formulation of Lagrange's method had been proposed by the Irish mathematician William Rowan Hamilton. Maxwell later used both forms but came to prefer Hamilton's because it more clearly demonstrated the relationship between the two basic quantities of a dynamical system—its energy and momentum. As usual, his intuition was right; it is

the Hamiltonian form that has become standard in many branches of modern physics.

6. When the equations are written in general form, rather than for the special case of empty space, they include extra terms for charge density and current density and for the electrical and magnetic characteristics of the material present. Even so, they are astonishingly simple.
7. For compactness, the equations of the electromagnetic field are shown in modern vector notation. This substitution is legitimate because Maxwell himself later began the process of modernisation. Even in modern guise the equations vary slightly according to the system of units used. I have chosen so-called Gaussian units, because they best illustrate the role of the constant c (the speed of light) as a kind of gear ratio between the electric and magnetic fields. In the Gaussian system, **E** is expressed in electrostatic units and **H** in electromagnetic units, so that c, or 1/c, serves as a conversion rate between the two. When, as is more usual, electromagnetic units are used throughout, 1/c disappears from equation (3), and $1/c^2$ replaces 1/c in equation (4). The Gaussian system of units was the first internationally accepted system of electrical units, adopted in 1881 at the Paris meeting of the Electrical Congress. As reported in the main narrative, Maxwell, not Gauss, was the chief contributor to this system of units.

   To avoid burdening the non-specialist reader with technicalities, I have used as few symbols as possible. It is usual to include extra vectors **B** and **D**. The equations then become:

$$\text{div } \mathbf{D} = 0 \qquad (1)$$

$$\text{div } \mathbf{B} = 0 \qquad (2)$$

$$\text{curl } \mathbf{E} = -(1/c)\ \partial\mathbf{B}/\partial t \qquad (3)$$

$$\text{curl } \mathbf{H} = (1/c)\ \partial\mathbf{D}/\partial t \qquad (4)$$

D is the density of the electric flux produced by the electric field intensity **E**. **B** is the density of the magnetic flux produced by

the magnetic field intensity **H**. But in Gaussian units, in the special case of empty space, **D** = **E** and **B** = **H**, allowing the equations to be written using **E** and **H** only.

8. **E** and **H** are, strictly speaking, not forces but rather the *intensities* of the electric and magnetic fields at our arbitrary point. They may, however, be thought of as forces waiting to act—specifically, the forces which *would* be exerted on, respectively, a unit charge or a unit magnetic pole if either were situated at the point.

9. In the *Dynamical Theory* paper, Maxwell expressed his results in rather more expansive form than that used here. It was more important to try to help people understand the new ideas than to put everything in a compact package. He gave eight equations of the electric and magnetic field, remarking that they might readily be condensed but that 'to eliminate a quantity which expresses a useful idea would be a loss rather than a gain at this stage of our enquiry'. One of the ideas thus expressed was Faraday's electrotonic state, which in Maxwell's scheme became the electromagnetic momentum of the field. He did condense the results in some later presentations.

   The paper contains an inconsistency in algebraic signs which has been much discussed by scholars. It is similar to the one in his *Physical Lines* paper and arises in the same context. Maxwell was wrestling with a chicken-and-egg question—does the electric charge cause the electric field or does the field cause the charge?—and seems to have taken different standpoints in different parts of the paper. Thomas K. Simpson gives a fuller account in his guided study, *Maxwell on the Electromagnetic Field*. Maxwell generally favoured primacy of the field, as Faraday had done, but some followers preferred to regard charge as the fundamental entity and their case was strengthened when the electron was discovered in 1897. Eventually the two viewpoints were reconciled in the formulation which is commonly taught today, a hybrid version which accords fundamental status to both field and charge; Daniel M. Siegel describes this process in *Innovation in Maxwell's Electromagnetic Theory*.

There is an interesting short note in the *Dynamical Theory* paper about gravitation. It was natural for Maxwell to see whether his idea that energy existed in empty space could somehow explain the gravitational field that caused attraction between bodies. He soon found that it could not, and presumably included the note to save others a trip down a blind alley. Maxwell, who loved to take a geometrical approach to problems wherever possible, would surely have delighted in Einstein's explanation that gravity is simply a manifestation of the geometry of space–time.

General note

Many years after Maxwell left King's College, a rumour got about that he had been asked to go because he could not keep order in his classes. It came from an apparently authoritative source, the 1928 centenary history of the College, but was later shown by Professor Cyril Domb and colleagues to have no foundation whatever. Astonishingly, the writer of the 'history' had reported and elaborated a reminiscence of 60 years before by someone who never knew Maxwell but thought he remembered hearing the story from someone else, who, it turned out, never knew Maxwell either and was never at King's College. Domb and his colleagues, who included the College archivist, found that almost every 'fact' reported was wrong. It seems that the writer had not even looked up the College's own records to check his sources. Domb gives a detailed account in his article listed in the bibliography.

Chapter 9 The Laird at home

1. The quotations beginning 'A man of middle height ... ' and 'He had a strong sense of humour ... ' are extracted from longer

quotations in Campbell and Garnett. The author of the remarks is not named.

2. Maxwell reported the results of his experiment to measure the ratio of the electromagnetic and electrostatic units of charge in *Method of Making a Direct Comparison of Electrostatic with Electromagnetic Force with a Note on the Electromagnetic Theory of Light*, published in 1868. As the title implies, this included the note on his electromagnetic theory, in which he criticised the rival theories of Weber and Riemann. Later, in his *Treatise on Electricity and Magnetism*, Maxwell compared his own and others' experimental results for the ratio of electrical units with the best direct measurements which had been made of the velocity of light in air or through space. His table reads:

Velocity of light (km/s)		Ratio of electrical units (km/s)	
Fizeau	314,000	Weber	310,740
Aberration etc. and sun's parallax	308,000	Maxwell	288,000
Fouceau	298,360	Thomson	282,000

Today's accepted value of the speed of light in a vacuum is 299,792.5 km/s.

3. *The Theory of Heat*, published in 1871, presented Maxwell's demon to the public, but the idea had already been talked and written about privately by Maxwell, Tait and Thomson. Maxwell's first recorded description of the demon is in a letter of 1867 to Tait.

4. Maxwell's demon facilitated a perpetual motion machine of the *second* kind. Whereas a machine of the first kind uses no energy, one of the second kind draws energy from neighbouring matter and will go on working until the temperature of that matter falls to absolute zero (−273° Celsius).

5. The letter in which Maxwell explains that most people's eyes have the yellow spot was to Cecil Monro. Campbell and Garnett give the full text of the letter.

6. The letter saying 'I have paid so little attention to the political sympathies of scientific men … ' was to W. R. Grove, who was vice-President of the Royal Institution. So far as he was political at all, Maxwell was a Conservative. The Conservatives lost the 1868 election and, as the narrative reports, by the time the Principalship of St Andrews was awarded, Gladstone's Liberal Party was in power.
7. The story of St Andrews turning down Joule is reported by R. V. Jones.

Chapter 10 The Cavendish

1. The quotation 'The human mind is seldom satisfied, and is certainly never exercising its highest functions, when it is doing the work of a calculating machine … ' is from Maxwell's presidential address to Section A of the British Association for the Advancement of Science in 1870.
2. Isaac Todhunter's reaction to being invited to witness conical refraction is reported by Arthur Schuster, one of Maxwell's students, in *The Progress of Physics*.
3. The author of the comment comparing Henry Cavendish's frequency of speech with that of Trappist monks was Henry Brougham, afterwards Lord Brougham, who, among other accomplishments, was instrumental in establishing University College, London.
4. The American visitor who took umbrage at being invited to use his body as a current meter was Samuel Pierpoint Langley, who invented the bolometer, a device for measuring radiant energy. C. G. Knott reports the incident in *The Life and Scientific Work of Peter Guthrie Tait*.
5. Maxwell's edition of Henry Cavendish's work was published in 1879 under the title *Electrical Writings of the Hon. Henry Cavendish*.

6. Maxwell's critical review of Guthrie's book *Practical Physics, Molecular Physics and Sound* was published by *Nature* in 1879. This review contained the passage 'If a child has any latent talent for the study of nature ... ', which is quoted in Chapter 3 in connection with James Forbes. The poem which begins 'Worry through duties academic ... ' has not, as far as I know, been included in any collection of Maxwell's poems. Naturally so, as he never acknowledged authorship—to have done so would, of course, have destroyed the joke. I am much indebted to Martin Goldman, who included the poem in his biography of Maxwell, *The Demon in the Aether*.
7. The quotation 'When the state of things is such that an infinitely small variation of the present state will alter ... ' is from an essay Maxwell wrote in 1873 for his essay group at Cambridge. The title is *Does the progress of Physical Science tend to give any advantage to the opinion of Necessity (or Determinism) over that of the contingency of events and the Freedom of the Will?* No doubt he would have shortened this for a wider audience, perhaps to *Science and Free Will*.
8. I have given the first and last of four verses of the poem *To the Committee of the Cayley Portrait Fund*. The full version can be found in Campbell and Garnett.
9. Maxwell's *Treatise on Electricity and Magnetism* has inspired many creative physicists and engineers. One of its most dedicated apostles was Oliver Heaviside, the maverick English virtuoso, who transformed telecommunications in 1887 by showing mathematically how to make a distortion-free telephone cable, and made other important innovations we now take for granted. Paul Nahin's biography is a treasure-house of information about Heaviside and his contemporaries and, concomitantly, about Maxwell's influence on their work.
10. For a while it was thought that Maxwell's radiation pressure was the main cause of comets' tails pointing away from the

sun. But in 1958, the American physicist Eugene Norman Parker demonstrated the existence of a 'solar wind' of particles thrown out by the sun and this is now believed to be the main influence on the behaviour of comets' tails. Nevertheless, radiation pressure plays a part.

11. The formula which Maxwell, Boltzmann and others used for the ratio of the specific heat of a gas at constant pressure to that at constant volume was:

$$\gamma = (n + 2)/n$$

where γ is the ratio of the specific heats and n is the number of independent modes of motion of the molecules into which energy can be transferred from molecule to molecule by jostling. The formula is based on the equipartition principle, by which kinetic energy becomes evenly spread over all the n modes of motion. The 2 on the top of the fraction represents the extra energy required for expansion when a gas is heated at constant pressure. (The value 2 derives from the work of the German physicist J. R. Mayer.) In his first paper on gas theory, Maxwell had assumed that molecules behaved like rough-surfaced billiard balls. When they collided they could transfer linear energy in three independent (x, y, z) directions and, being rough-surfaced, could also transfer their rotational energy, again in three independent directions. So Maxwell's first value for γ was $(6 + 2)/6 = 4/3 = 1.333$, whereas experiments gave 1.408. When n was later increased to take into account vibrational modes of molecular motion the theoretical value of γ, already too low, decreased and the discrepancy grew. Things got even worse when further results from spectroscopy suggested that a gas could have many different modes of vibrational motion.

12. The paucity of information about Katherine and about the domestic life she shared with James is a source of much frustration for anyone with an interest in Maxwell. He wrote

to her every day when they were apart and it is a pity that Lewis Campbell did not include more of the letters in his biography. He gave us a few letters, some matter-of-fact, some pious, but held back a much larger number of light-hearted ones, which were since lost. To compound our frustration, he tells us what we are missing:

> ... letters full of '*enfantillages*', as in his boyish endeavours to amuse his father, telling her of everything, however minute, which, if she had seen it, would have detained her eye, small social phenomena, grotesque or graceful (including the dress of lady friends), together with the lighter aspects of the examinations; College customs, such as the 'grace-cup'; his dealings with his co-examiners, and marks of honour to himself which he knew would please her, though they were indifferent to him.

How much better informed we might have been. But it would be churlish to complain: thanks to Campbell we have a substantial, if not quite complete, picture of Maxwell the man. As for Katherine, there is little to go on beyond what appears in the main narrative. Maxwell's female relations seem, on the whole, to have disliked her, as do his colleagues and their wives, but some of their comments can, as we have seen, be taken with more than a pinch of salt.

General note

When Maxwell died, the University once again invited William Thomson to accept the Cavendish professorship, and again he decided to stay in Glasgow. The post went to Lord Rayleigh, a 37 year-old Essex gentleman who had built a laboratory next to his manor house. A fine and underrated physicist, he is now remembered chiefly for explaining the scattering of light that makes the sky blue and for discovering argon, jointly with William Ramsay. Nine years earlier, as plain J. W. Strutt, he had been foremost among the young Cambridge dons who entreated Maxwell to return to Cambridge. Rayleigh consolidated the Cavendish's good start before retiring to his country laboratory in 1884. As proprietor of Lord Rayleigh's dairies he had developed an acute business acumen which he brought to bear by setting the Cavendish's finances on a more secure base, starting an apparatus fund to which he contributed generously himself. He also introduced systematic training in laboratory techniques, moving on from Maxwell's *laisser faire* approach. The next two professors between them ran the Cavendish until 1939. They were J. J. Thomson, who discovered the electron, and Ernest Rutherford, who discovered the basic structure of the atom.

Chapter 11 Last days

1. William Garnett, Maxwell's demonstrator at the Cavendish, who visited him at Glenlair in September 1879, collaborated with Lewis Campbell to write *The Life of James Clerk Maxwell.* While Campbell wrote the main biographical narrative, Garnett acted as researcher and compiler of material and wrote a 110 page section on Maxwell's contributions to science. Garnett's report is, not surprisingly, hopelessly inadequate from our perspective—nobody at the time had a proper grasp of the immense significance of Maxwell's work. The juxtaposition of extracts from Maxwell's papers with Garnett's own prose provides an interesting contrast: Maxwell dances where Garnett plods. But Garnett's admiration, and indeed love, for the great man shine through and the account has charm as well as historical interest.
2. The full text of Dr Butler's address at Maxwell's memorial service is given in Campbell and Garnett. Butler later became Master of Trinity College, where he and Maxwell had met as students.

Chapter 12 Maxwell's legacy

1. Some readers may welcome a little more background to Maxwell's part in the genesis of Einstein's *Special Theory of Relativity*.

Michelson and Morley carried out their famous experiment in Cleveland, Ohio, in 1887. They wanted to detect and measure the 'aether drift'—the motion of the earth through the substance called the aether which was thought to permeate all space and to be the medium by which light waves were transmitted. Maxwell himself had worked out the great accuracy required to do this and doubted whether it could be achieved in any laboratory. He had set out his reasons in a letter to David Peck Todd at the Nautical Almanac Office in Washington, together with a suggestion for an alternative method using observations on Jupiter's moons. When Maxwell died a few months later Todd had the letter published. Nothing much came of the Jupiter scheme but when Michelson saw Maxwell's letter he took the great man's doubts about earthbound methods as a challenge and over the next 8 years developed his interferometer—an instrument which used the tiny wavelengths of light itself as measurement units and so made possible a degree of precision formerly unthought of. With the help of his colleague Morley, Michelson then set out to measure the difference in the speed of the two parts of a light beam split at right angles. This difference would determine the aether drift.

The instrument was amply accurate for its purpose but, to the experimenters' consternation, the speed of light in both directions was identical. Repeated attempts gave the same result. This was a great disappointment and at first the experiment was seen by the scientific community as no more than another failed attempt to detect the aether drift. Michelson himself seldom mentioned his result and never recognised its immense significance. But others began to see that here was some new and important evidence and put forward ideas to account for it. The Irishman George Francis Fitzgerald proposed that all objects moving through the aether contract along the direction of movement just sufficiently to make the aether drift undetectable, and produced a formula for the contraction. His formula implied that any object which approached the speed of light would appear to be squashed flat. Fitzgerald's associates thought he had gone mad, but, in Holland, Hendrik Antoon Lorentz independently came up with the same formula and a complementary one, by which movement through the aether makes clocks slow down. Astonishingly, these modifications to space and time seemed to be intrinsic to Maxwell's equations of the electromagnetic field: they worked perfectly under Lorentz's transformation. But Newton's laws of motion, which had been the bedrock of all calculations on moving bodies, did not.

Here was a crisis; leading theorists searched for an explanation. Some, including Lorentz and the great French mathematician Henri Poincaré, came close but it was Albert Einstein who solved the puzzle with a masterly shaft of insight. Despite what our senses tell us, there are no absolute measures of space or time; all are relative. The only absolute quantity is the speed of light, which is the same for all observers in unaccelerated motion, no matter how fast or in what direction they are moving. And the speed of light is completely determined by Maxwell's theory: his equations are the very core of special relativity, providing the link between space and time.

What of the aether? At first, Einstein, like everyone else, had thought that an aether of some kind was necessary for the transmission of light; but it would need to operate in absolute space and time, and when he demolished those there was no longer a home, or need, for the aether; in their new guise, space and time had themselves taken on the role.

Michelson and Morley's experiment is now recognised as one of the most important in the history of physics. It

handsomely bears out Maxwell's philosophy: 'I never try to dissuade a man from trying an experiment; if he does not find what he wants he may find out something else'.

2. The prediction from (classical) theory that matter should radiate away all its kinetic energy came to be known as 'the ultraviolet catastrophe', as the problem lay at the high-frequency end of the radiation spectrum, where the 'classical' formula for the energy of radiation diverged. Readers with mathematical training will find a fascinating account of the genesis of quantum theory, and much more, in Malcolm Longair's superb book *Theoretical Concepts in Physics*.
3. Lewis Campbell paints a moving pen-picture of his lifelong friend in the closing chapter of Campbell and Garnett. It is here that he writes: 'The leading note of Maxwell's character is a grand simplicity'.

BIBLIOGRAPHY

Note: Some of the publications of Maxwell that are mentioned in the narrative are listed below under their own titles. The others can be found in the collections of his writings edited by Niven and by Harman, also listed.

Bell, E. T. *Men of Mathematics*, 2 vols., Penguin Books, Harmondsworth (reprinted 1965).

Blackburn, J. (Ed. Rob Fairley). *Jemima: The Paintings and Memoirs of a Victorian Lady*. Canongate, Edinburgh (1988).

Campbell, L. and Garnett, W. *The Life of James Clerk Maxwell*. Macmillan, London (1882; 2nd edition 1884).

Cannell, D. M. *George Green, Mathematician and Physicist, 1793–1841*. Athlone Press, London (1993).

Community Council of Kirkpatrick Durham. *James Clerk Maxwell: Pathfinder of Modern Science, A Centenary Tribute* (1979).

Domb, C. (Ed.). *Clerk Maxwell and Modern Science*. Athlone Press, London (1963).

Domb, C. Clerk Maxwell in London 1860–1865. *Notes and Records of the Royal Society of London*, 1980, **35**(1).

Dyson, F. J. Why is Maxwell's theory so hard to understand? Article in the *James Clerk Maxwell Foundation's Commemorative Booklet*. Edinburgh (1999).

Einstein, A. Maxwell's Influence on the Development of the Conception of Reality. Essay in *James Clerk Maxwell, A Commemoration Volume*. Cambridge University Press, Cambridge (1931).

Everitt, C. W. F. *James Clerk Maxwell: Physicist and Natural Philosopher*. Charles Scribner's Sons, New York (1975).

Everitt, C. W. F. Maxwell's Scientific Papers. *Applied Optics*, 1967, **6**(4).

Feynmann, R. P., Leighton, R. B. and Sands, M. *Lectures on Physics*. Addison-Wesley, New York (1965).

Fleming, A. Some memories. Essay in *James Clerk Maxwell, A Commemoration Volume*. Cambridge University Press, Cambridge (1931).

Forfar, D. O. Generations of genius. Article in the *James Clerk Maxwell Foundation's Commemorative Booklet*. Edinburgh (1999).

Forfar, D. O. and Pritchard, C. The remarkable story of Maxwell and Tait. Article in the *James Clerk Maxwell Foundation's Commemorative Booklet*. Edinburgh (1999).

Garnett, W. Maxwell's Laboratory. Essay in *James Clerk Maxwell, A Commemoration Volume*. Cambridge University Press, Cambridge (1931).

Glazebrook, R. T. *James Clerk Maxwell and Modern Physics*. Cassell, London (1901).

Glazebrook, R. T. *Early days at the Cavendish laboratory*. Essay in *James Clerk Maxwell, A Commemoration Volume*. Cambridge University Press, Cambridge (1931).

Goldman, M., *The Demon in the Aether: The Life of James Clerk Maxwell*. Paul Harris Publishing, Edinburgh (1983).

Harman, P. M. *The Natural Philosophy of James Clerk Maxwell*. Cambridge University Press, Cambridge (1998).

Harman, P. M. (Ed.), *The Scientific Papers and Letters of James Clerk Maxwell*, 3 vols., Cambridge University Press, Cambridge (1990, 1995, 2002).

Hoffmann, B. *The Strange Story of the Quantum*. Penguin Books, Harmondsworth (1963).

James Clerk Maxwell Foundation. *James Clerk Maxwell Foundation's Commemorative Booklet*. Edinburgh (1999).

Jeans, J. James Clerk Maxwell's Method. Essay in *James Clerk Maxwell, A Commemoration Volume*. Cambridge University Press (1931).

Jones, R. V. The Complete Physicist: James Clerk Maxwell 1831–1879. *Yearbook of the Royal Society of Edinburgh*. Edinburgh (1980).

Knott, C. G. *Life and Scientific Work of Peter Guthrie Tait*. Cambridge University Press, Cambridge (1911).

Lamb, H. *Clerk Maxwell as Lecturer*. Essay in *James Clerk Maxwell, A Commemoration Volume*. Cambridge University Press, Cambridge (1931).

Larmor, J. The Scientific Environment of James Clerk Maxwell. Essay in *James Clerk Maxwell, A Commemoration Volume*. Cambridge University Press, Cambridge (1931).

Leff, H. S. and Rex, A. F. (Ed.). *Maxwell's Demon: Entropy, Information, Computing*. Adam Hilger, Bristol (1990).

Lodge, O. Clerk Maxwell and the Wireless Telegraph. Essay in *James Clerk Maxwell, A Commemoration Volume*. Cambridge University Press, Cambridge (1931).

Longair, M. S. *Theoretical Concepts in Physics*. Cambridge University Press, Cambridge (1984).

Maxwell, J. C. *A Treatise on Electricity and Magnetism*, 2 vol., 3rd edn. Clarendon Press, Oxford (re-published 1998).

Maxwell, J. C. *Theory of Heat*. Longmans, Green and Co., London (1871).

Maxwell, J. C. *Matter and Motion*. Notes and appendices by Joseph Larmor. Republished by Dover Publications, New York (1991).

Maxwell, J. C. *A Dynamical Theory of the Electromagnetic Field*, edited and introduced by T.F. Torrance. Scottish Academic Press, Edinburgh (1982).

Nahin, P. J. *Oliver Heaviside, Sage in Solitude*. IEEE Press, New York (1988).

Niven, W. D. (Ed.). *The Scientific Papers of James Clerk Maxwell*, 2 vols. Cambridge University Press, Cambridge (1890).

Penrose, R. *The Emperor's New Mind*. Oxford University Press, New York (1989; and Vintage, London, 1990).

Planck, M. Maxwell's influence on theoretical physics in Germany. Essay in *James Clerk Maxwell, A Commemoration Volume*. Cambridge University Press, Cambridge (1931).

Pritchard, C. Aspects of the life and work of Peter Guthrie Tait. Article in the *James Clerk Maxwell Foundation's Commemorative Booklet*. Edinburgh (1999).

Sagan, C. *The Demon-haunted World: Science as a Candle in the Dark*. Headline, London (1995).

Schuster, A. *The Progress of Physics*. Cambridge University Press, Cambridge (1911).

Siegel, D. M. *Innovation in Maxwell's Electromagnetic Theory*. Cambridge University Press, Cambridge (1991).

Simpson, T. K. *Maxwell on the Electromagnetic Field*. Rutgers University Press, New Brunswick, NJ (1997).

Reid, J. S. James Clerk Maxwell's Scottish Chair. Article in the *James Clerk Maxwell Foundation's Commemorative Booklet*. Cambridge (1999).

Thomson, J. J. James Clerk Maxwell. Essay in *James Clerk Maxwell, A Commemoration Volume*. Cambridge University Press, Cambridge (1931).

Tolstoy, I. *James Clerk Maxwell: A Biography*. Canongate, Edinburgh (1981).

Tolstoy, I. *The Knowledge and the Power: Reflections on the History of Science*. Canongate, Edinburgh (1990).

Weart, S. R. and Phillips, M. (Eds). *History of Physics*. American Institute of Physics, New York (1985).

Whittaker, E. T. *A History of the Theories of Aether and Electricity*. Thomas Nelson and Sons, London (1951; republished by Dover Publications, New York, 1989).

INDEX

INDEX